S0-AFB-548

THE Sign OF THE KINGDOM

"Then shall appear the sign of the Son of Man in heaven…"

— Matthew 24:30 KJV

THE
Sign
OF THE
KINGDOM

The Present Reign of Christ
In Light of the Olivet Discourse

George E. Kouri
Richard Hogue

LIBRARY
WILLOW MEADOWS BAPTIST CHURCH
9999 GREENWILLOW
HOUSTON, TEXAS 77035

9421

Published by

AMI
Apostolic Ministries International

Published by

Apostolic Ministries International

1998

Unless otherwise noted, all sited Scriptures references are from the
New American Standard Bible

check footnotes for underlined book titles

Copyright © 1998 by George E. Kouri & Richard Hogue.
All rights reserved.

Jacket design and typography by Mark E. Kouri

No portion of this book may be reproduced, stored in a retrieval system,
or transmitted in any form or by any means—electronic, mechanical,
photographic, recording, or any other—except for brief quotations in
printed reviews, without the prior permission of the publisher.

ISBN 0–9662–5761–8

Printed in the United States of America

CONTENTS

ACKNOWLEDGMENTS

We would like to express profound appreciation and thanks to the following for their contributions, encouragement and indulgence in this project:

Our wives—Sandra Kouri and Marilyn Hogue—thanks for being there to encourage us to get this book written.

Our production team—Kenneth Jennison, editor; Matthew Ryan Duck, footnotes and research assistant; Jon A. Lusk publishing consultant & editing; Michal Lusk, proofreading; Mark E. Kouri, editing and publication design—thanks for being personally involved for countless hours in this endeavor.

This book is lovingly and gratefully dedicated
to the memory of

W. J. E. (Ern) Baxter.

Brother Baxter was a rugged and courageous pioneer
among evangelical, pentecostal, and charismatic leaders
of the twentieth century in the recovery of a truly
Biblical understanding of the Kingdom of God, the
New Testament Church, and Apostolic Ministry. His
monumental knowledge of the Holy Scriptures together
with his extraordinary depth of insight and
understanding of the mysteries of the Kingdom of God
made him a giant among the servants of God of this
century. Also, his prophetic sensitivity to the present
move of the Holy Spirit coupled with his uncommon
grasp of the immense issues facing the Church as it
moves into the twenty-first century made him a voice
crying in the wilderness,
"prepare the way of the Lord!"

INTRODUCTION

The Church enters the 21st century with a great deal of confusion about the future. The Sign of the Kingdom was written to help the Church understand the future, and define its mission and destiny. In order to fully understand what lies ahead, it is necessary to reach back and focus once again on the teaching Jesus gave thousands of years ago during His Olivet Discourse.

The Olivet Discourse is about Jesus and His Kingdom. It is His word, His teaching, and His prophetic promise. It is arguably the most important and comprehensive passage of scripture in the entire Bible. Just a few days before His crucifixion, standing on the Mount of Olives, Jesus clearly presented His eschatology. The Lord laid out the divine chronology for the unfolding of His Messianic Kingdom throughout the Christian era. He detailed the pattern of judgment that would characterize His government over the nations. A government that would begin with His resurrection, ascension, enthronement, and glorious outpouring of the Holy Spirit on the day of Pentecost, and continuing until His triumphant Second Coming at the end of history.

The Olivet Discourse records Jesus' personal commentary on and explanation of the only prophecy He gave in the entire New Testament. It also records the Lord's very specific declarations concerning the nature and timing of the single cataclysmic historical event which He said would be the fulfillment of His prophecy and the sign to the nations of the present reign of the Son of Man in heaven.

In the Olivet Discourse the Lord Jesus gave the original Apostles His understanding and interpretation of the eschatology of the Kingdom. His eschatology would be the fulfillment of the Old Testament; not only its prophecies, but its types and shadows. As has been seen throughout history, if the Church does not understand or accept Jesus' eschatology it is tempted to invent its own. Tragically, this has occurred many times throughout the history of the Church, causing great misunderstanding concerning the nature and purpose of the present reign of Christ. In addition, it has caused much confusion, conflict, and division among God's people concerning the true nature of the Church and its purpose and mission in history.

Many mistakenly think the study of eschatology is impractical and therefore unimportant. Others believe it only leads to endless controversy and confusion. Nothing could be further from the truth. While it is true the convoluted and complicated eschatologies of men and their theological systems bring confusion causing strife and division, the Olivet Discourse is the eschatology of the Lord Jesus Christ Himself. It provided the foundation of the preaching and teaching of the original Apostles. It was the basis of the early Church's faith and confidence. And unless we properly understand and correctly interpret its message, we will not properly understand the reality and divine purpose of the present reign of God's anointed King. We will not understand what the Lord is doing today or how His Kingdom works. Nor will we understand the Church's true identity, mission, or destiny as the community and instrument of the Kingdom.

As we stand on the threshold of a new millennium, looking at a world desperately in need of the government of God, this is no time for confusion or division!

This book is not intended to be controversial or divisive. Rather, it seeks to resolve controversy, remove confusion, and restore unity to Christ's Kingdom community by allowing the eschatology of the Lord Jesus to come into clear focus. It is the authors' deepest desire and fervent prayer that *The Sign of the Kingdom* will help the Lord's Church understand the present reign of God's anointed King, so that as members of His body, we might better understand who we are in Him and rise up together and fulfill our purpose and destiny as the people of God.

THE SIGN OF THE KINGDOM

1

THE SETTING OF THE SIGN

The streets of Jerusalem were filled to overflowing. All Jewish men living within twenty miles of the city were required to be present. During the following days, more than 250,000 lambs would be sacrificed by the 2,500,000 Jewish faithful who had gathered from across the populated earth to celebrate Passover week.

Despite the crowds, that Sunday morning was routine. People were making their regular rounds when the distant sound of singing slowly rolled over Jerusalem. Commotion began to fill the city. Soon hundreds were streaming out of the city to join a growing multitude of Galileans coming toward Jerusalem from the Mount of Olives. The central figure in this strange procession was a solitary man riding a small donkey. The two crowds merged at the summit of the mount. With boisterous fervor the multitude escorted the colt and its rider toward Jerusalem. As the exuberant praises grew continually louder the attention of the entire city was drawn to this celebration which was entering the eastern gate of Jerusalem.

Singing, shouting, dancing, the multitude ripped branches off trees, removed their garments and threw them across the path of a donkey on which rode one they believed to be the Messiah–the Son of David. Shouting at the top of their collective voices, this profusion of worshippers screamed out to the heavens: "Hosanna to the Son of David! Blessed is He who comes in the name of the Lord! Hosanna in the highest!"

Their praises were easily recognized by every Jew in Jerusalem. They were Messianic songs. The entire city erupted with excitement. Expectant energy passed from person to person. Could this be the great Messianic moment for which the nation had prayed and believed for thousands of years? Were the promises of the Prophets finally coming true before their very eyes? Everyone in the city was scurrying, pushing, fighting their way through the crowd to find a way to view this possible Messiah.

Jerusalem had seen very little of Jesus. He had purposely avoided the city. As the throng pushed its way through the narrow confines of the Eastern Gate, questions were hurled at the celebrants:

"Who is this?" (Matthew 21:10) the city asked.
The multitude of admirers shouted back:
"This is the prophet Jesus!" (Matthew 21:11)

There was nothing accidental concerning this triumphant entry into Jerusalem. Jesus acted with evident intention and unquestioned authority. He meticulously arranged the entire event. He sent His disciples to find the colt knowing both its location and the mind-set of the owners of the beast. Carefully, deliberately, and with great purpose He orchestrated each aspect of the day to precisely fulfill the prophetic demands upon the entrance of Messiah:

"Say to the daughters of Zion,
Behold your king is coming to you,

Gentle, and mounted on a donkey,
Even on a colt, the foal of a beast of burden."
(Matthew 21:5)

Matthew saw the detailed actions of Jesus fulfilling the vision of Zechariah. The Prophet had seen the donkey, the entry, the excited multitude, and ultimately the rejection and death of the anointed King.

When Jesus rode into Jerusalem the expectant nation was His for the taking. The Messianic hope of Israel was high. They were intensely looking for the Son of David to destroy the Roman occupation and restore the glory of Israel.

Williston Walker, former professor of Church history at Yale University, describes in detail the Jewish hope and expectation:

"By the time of Christ [the Jewish hope] involved the destruction of Roman authority by supernatural divine intervention through a Messiah; and the establishment of a kingdom of God in which a freed and all-powerful Judaism should flourish under a righteous Messianic King of Davidic descent, into which the Jews scattered throughout the Roman Empire should be gathered, and by which a golden age would be begun." [1]

Renowned dispensational theologian J. Dwight Pentecost agrees:

"The [Jewish] hope was for an earthly kingdom." [2]

Jesus had indeed come to establish a Kingdom, but not the earthly Kingdom the crowds were expecting. He had not

---

1 Williston Walker, A History of the Christian Church, (New York: Charles Scribner's Sons, 1945), p. 15.
2 J. Dwight Pentecost, Things to Come: A Study in Biblical Eschatology, (Grand Rapids: Zondervan), p. 108.

entered Jerusalem hoping to find acceptance for a restored physical Davidic Kingdom. Despite the accolades of the people, His purpose was set. The outcome had been determined before the foundations of the world. Noted theologian G. Campbell Morgan concurs:

"He did not yield Himself to the popular clamour, but He evoked the popular clamour, and that of set and deliberate purpose." [3]

Jesus' purpose was established. He, Himself, provoked the demonstration and deliberately planned every detail of the entrance to attract Jerusalem to the fact of His coming. He had often passed into Jerusalem quietly. However, once, and once only, He entered in such a way as to manifest the fact of His Kingship and His meekness to the crowds of Jerusalem. He demanded that Jerusalem recognize Him at least for an hour, at least until the nation had heard His voice again, and at least until they had seen His authority once more. It worked:

"All the city was stirred!" (Matthew 21:10)

Throughout this final week and climaxing with the Olivet Discourse, Jesus' message to the nation was not one of hope, but one of judgment. Jerusalem was not about to be delivered, but destroyed. Messiah's Kingdom would not bring new glory to the nation, but remove her former glory and leave her desolate.

Jesus had come to reject the nation. Morgan observes:

"The King is seen deliberately passing back to Jerusalem for the express purpose of definitely and officially rejecting the Hebrew nation. It is the story of the rejection of the Hebrew nation by the King, not that of the rejection of the King by the nation." [4]

3 G. Campbell Morgan, <u>Studies in the Four Gospels</u>, (Old Tappan, NJ: Flemming H. Revell, 1931), p. 249.
4 Morgan, p. 248.

However, many teachers insist that Jesus came to earth to establish an earthly, political, Jewish Kingdom. If that were so, then His triumphant entry into Jerusalem was His grand opportunity! Yet, He did not do so.

Ironically, as we enter the twenty-first century, the Church is being told to expect Jesus to do the very thing He refused to do that day. Today, much of the Church is transfixed upon a theology which insists upon an earthly, political, Jewish Kingdom as the ultimate will of God, and the ultimate purpose of the ministry of the Lord Jesus.

Unaware of the consequences, millions of Christians believe this distorted teaching. By doing so, they not only rob the Church of its purpose and victory, but they misconstrue the genuine person and work of the Lord Jesus. It would logically follow that a failure to properly understand who Jesus was and now is would of necessity produce a distorted understanding of why He came to earth.

Yet, what did Jesus do? He did not ride into the city astride a magnificent white stallion as a conquering political king would have demanded. Instead, He mounted upon the colt of a common donkey. Furthermore, He did not ride His humble mount to the palace of Herod to overthrow Israel's civil leadership. Instead, He rode His lowly beast to His own palace—the place where His honor was to dwell. He rode to the Temple, the nation's monument to the government of God.

J. W. Hodges, the great Princeton scholar, correctly declares:

> "...To claim that Messiah's mission to earth, even in part, was to bolster the sagging political fortunes of national Israel is the height of folly and doctrinal error." [5]

When Jesus arrived at the Temple He did not enter to receive their accolades as a political king or foment rebellion

5 Jesse Wilson Hodges, Christ's Kingdom and Its Coming, (Grand Rapids: Wm. B. Eerdmans, 1957), p. 109.

against the Roman occupation. He had not come to be their earthly national king; but rather, He entered to demonstrate with overwhelming symbolism that His unequivocal Messianic mission was to bring judgment upon the entire society of Israel. That judgment would begin in the House of God. Soon, it would engulf the nation and, from Jerusalem, cover the earth with the saving rule of His Kingdom.

The house of God needed cleansing. The Temple was despicable! Literally, it was a "den of thieves."

The sacrificial system of the Temple had become completely corrupt. What was intended to be the worship of Jehovah had been reduced to a profit-driven business which stole from the people and enriched the High Priest and his family. The financial business of the sacrifices had taken over the Temple. The Temple officials required offerings to be made with local coins which necessitated the exchange of the money of foreign Jews and proselytes. In order to meet the requirement for local coins, money changers' tables lined the entrance of the eastern gate, and filled Solomon's Porch. These money changers were agents of the High Priest, and they took great advantage of the people with illegal exchange rates. Through the hands of these money changers passed the equivalent of millions of dollars each year. The business of the Temple sacrifices had become very profitable—a profit enjoyed by the High Priest and his family.

Josephus, the renowned Jewish historian who lived in Jerusalem during Jesus' earthly ministry, describes Annas, the son of the High Priest of the New Testament as:

"...'a great hoarder up of money', very rich, and as despoiling by open violence the common priests of their official revenues (Antiq. 20.9.2-4)."[6]

---

6 Alfred Edersheim, The Life and Times of Jesus the Messiah, 2 vols. in one, (1994; 2nd reprint ed., Peabody, MA: Hendrickson, 1993), part one p. 372.

It was not uncommon for the servants of the High Priests to beat with sticks those who refused to accept their illegal and immoral financial activities.

The noted Church historian Alfred Edersheim writes detailed volumes of the desecration which was taking place in the Sanctuary during the life of Jesus:

> "We can picture to ourselves the scene around the table of an Eastern money changer—the weighing of the coins, deductions for loss of weight, arguing, disputing, bargaining—and we can realize the terrible truthfulness of our Lord's charge that they had made the Father's House a mart and place of traffic... The whole of this traffic—money changing, selling of doves, and market for sheep and oxen—was in itself, and from its attendant circumstances, a terrible desecration; it was also liable to gross abuses." [7]

Earlier, in the very beginning of His ministry Jesus had seen the abuse of the Temple system. His response had been immediate. Making a scourge of cords, He drove the money changers out of the Temple declaring:

> "Take these things away; stop making My Father's house a house of merchandise." (John 2:16)

As He returned to the Temple during the last week of His earthly life, Jesus once again encountered the desecration and was filled with righteous rage. He seized the money changers' tables and tossed them across the floor of the court. Evoking the words of Isaiah and Jeremiah, He destroyed the seats of those selling doves, declaring:

> "My house shall be called a house of prayer, but you have made it a robbers' den." (Matthew 21:13)

7 Edersheim, pp. 222-256.

Triumphantly, the Lord entered His own city, went to His Father's house and demonstrated His authority. No one dared challenge Him. The crowds knew He was correct in what He was doing. Many of them had been the victims of the Temple abuse. By His authority, the Temple was cleansed of the unrighteous merchandising of the priesthood; and, at least for the moment, it was restored to the service of His Father. As the robbers were forced to leave, Jesus began to speak.

People gathered from throughout the Temple Mount—the poor, the suffering, those who desperately needed a touch from this Miracle Messiah. In the midst of the fury of that moment, He paused *to heal the blind and the lame*. At each step, He was demanding that the nation recognize Him. He operated with sheer Messianic power. Demonstration after demonstration, there could no longer be any question. He was the triumphant Son of David, the promised Messiah. As He moved from the money changers to the miracles, the crowd filled the Temple with continual declarations of "HOSANNA TO THE SON OF DAVID!"

The Chief Priest and scribes were livid. They thought He had—with His heresy—intruded upon their source of power and fortune. Besides, they had long since rejected the idea of a suffering Messiah who would bring repentance and salvation to Israel. Their hope was for a king with political and military power. Nothing less would suffice. The Chief Priest and scribes expected Him to be beating up Romans, not cleaning out the Temple. Indignantly they turned on Him and demanded:

"Do you hear what these are saying?" (Matthew 21:16)

His immediate reply was both dramatic and prophetic as Jesus drew upon the Psalm of David:

"Yes; have you not read, 'Out of the mouth of nursing babes Thou hast prepared praise for Thyself'?" (Matthew 21:16)

What an extraordinary way to begin the final week of His physical life. During these seven last days, Messianic prophecies were fulfilled all around Him. On His way to the cross, He repeatedly confronted Jerusalem and its apostate religious leadership. For He had not come to the city that week to enjoy their hospitality nor to seek their approval, but to declare and complete their judgment. He had come to leave their city desolate. He had come to the city to declare unequivocally that Jerusalem and its Temple were doomed. Before the lives of that particular generation would be completed, the nation would be destroyed. His coming to Jerusalem was an inescapable promise of a day of judgment. This was the setting for His Olivet Discourse.

Jesus' every move during His final week was directed by the Prophets.

Nearly 450 years earlier, Malachi predicted the day of His coming. The Day of the Lord would be a day in which the judgment of heaven would fall upon all unrighteousness. Contrary to what many mistakenly believe, there would be no prophetic word of delay or postponement once the way was prepared. Malachi boldly declared:

"And the Lord, whom you seek, will suddenly come
to His Temple; and the messenger of the covenant,
in whom you delight, behold, He is coming, says the
Lord of hosts." (Malachi 3:1)

The "day of His coming" which Malachi saw was in no way a day of political intrigue or nation-building. It was a day of judgment:

"But who can endure the day of His coming? And who can stand when He appears? For He is like a refiner's fire and like fullers' soap. And He will sit as a smelter and purifier of silver..." (Malachi 3:2-3)

"'I will draw near to you for judgment; and I will be a swift witness against the sorcerers and against the adulterers and against those who swear falsely, and against those who oppress the wage earner in his wages, the widow and the orphan, and those who turn aside the alien, and do not fear Me,' says the Lord of Hosts." (Malachi 3:5)

"For behold, the day is coming, burning like a furnace; and all the arrogant and every evildoer will be chaff; and the day that is coming will set them ablaze, says the Lord of hosts, so that it will leave them neither root nor branch." (Malachi 4:1)

As Jesus cleansed the Temple, He was symbolically warning Israel of their coming judgment at His hands.

Leaving the city late Sunday afternoon, Jesus walked the two miles to Bethany, probably spending the night with the family of Lazarus. As He returned to the city very early Monday morning, His message had not changed. In fact, it had intensified. The judgment of the nation would be swift, severe, and forever. Along the road to Jerusalem He encountered a fruitless fig tree:

"'No longer shall there ever be any fruit from you.'
And at once the fig tree withered." (Matthew 21:19)

Condemning the fruitless tree, Jesus was prophetically condemning the fruitless nation. Edersheim explains the symbolism:

"Israel was that barren fig tree; and the leaves only
covered their nakedness...the judgment, symbolically
spoken in the Parable, must be symbolically executed
in this leafy fig-tree, barren when searched for fruit
by the Master." [8]

The severity of Jesus' judgment was obvious:

"No longer shall there ever be any fruit on you..."
(Matthew 21:19)

The judgment was forever. Natural Israel would never
again be the covenantal people of God.

The disciples marveled; how could the fig tree wither
immediately? The Lord's answer to His disciples would prove
to be the greatest challenge of their lives:

"If you have faith, and do not doubt, you shall not
only do what was done to the fig tree, but even if
you say to this mountain, 'Be taken up and be cast
into the sea,' it shall happen." (Matthew 21: 21)

Jesus was preparing His disciples. The mountain which
they would cast into the sea would be the mountain of
Jerusalem. Ultimately, the Messianic judgment, which King
Jesus had prophesied would fall upon the nation, would be
the result of the faith and prophetic prayers of the disciples.

Throughout this final week, culminating in the Olivet
Discourse, His prophetic message remained unchanged.
Apostate Israel was about to be destroyed, and she would
never again be fruitful.

Upon arriving at the Temple Monday morning, the Chief
Priest and elders directly confronted Him, demanding to
know the authority by which He was healing the sick and
speaking with such power. Jesus answered them with a series

---

8 Edersheim, p. 732.

of three parables. Woven throughout the parables were the strongest denunciations Jesus ever made. He was prophesying pure Messianic Kingdom judgment upon the nation.

He first spoke of two sons. The righteous son was determined by his obedience, not outward piety and verbiage. The message was strident. The sons of the Kingdom would be known by their obedience to the King. Jesus turned upon the religious leadership of the nation and declared:

> "Truly I say to you that the tax-gatherers and harlots
> will get into the kingdom of God before you."
> (Matthew 21:31)

The theme of judgment against the nation and its leadership continues in the parable of the landowner who planted a vineyard and rented it out to wretches who would not pay him his rent. After the unfaithful renters kill the landowner's son, the landowner returns, destroys the wretches and finds new renters for his vineyard.

The Lord's message was direct. Israel and its leaders would kill the Son of God, and God would come in judgment, remove them from His vineyard, and find faithful renters who would produce the fruit of the Kingdom. Even the apostate religious leadership of Israel understood the Lord's parable. When Jesus asked what the landowner should do to the wicked renters, they replied, pronouncing judgment upon themselves:

> "He will bring those wretches to a wretched end, and
> will rent out the vineyard to other vinegrowers, who
> will pay him the proceeds at the proper seasons."
> (Matthew 21:41)

They were right!

Immediately, Jesus made His most emphatic statement concerning the future of national Israel and the Kingdom of God:

> "Therefore I say to you, the kingdom of God shall be taken away from you, and given to a nation producing the fruit of it." (Matthew 21:43)

Dr. Herschel Hobbs, the renowned Southern Baptist scholar explains:

> "The word "you" (humon) is plural. So Jesus' words included not simply the rulers but the nation which they represented." [9]

Jesus could not have made a stronger declaration. The leaders of the nation understood completely. The Kingdom for which they had longed and expected for millennia would never be theirs. They were so incensed by His announcement that they immediately wanted to kill Him, but they feared the crowd. The crowd knew Jesus was a prophet. They knew He was speaking the truth of God.

Taking Jesus at face value, the Kingdom of God would be taken away from physical Israel and given to a new people—the Church of Jesus Christ. In all of this, the Lord was setting the stage for His Olivet Discourse.

Jesus continued His parables, speaking next of a king who had given a wedding feast for his son. The king sent his servants to inform the invited guests that everything was ready–"come to the feast!" Yet, no one would come:

> "They paid no attention and went their own way, one to his own farm, another to his business, and the rest seized his slaves and mistreated them and killed them." (Matthew 22:5-6)

---

9 Herschel H. Hobbs, <u>An Exposition of the Four Gospels: Volume 1 The Gospel of Matthew</u>, four volumes, (Nashville: Broadman, 1965), p. 299.

Jesus then made a remarkable prophetic statement in the midst of the parable:

> "The king was enraged and sent his armies, and
> destroyed those murderers, and set their city on fire."
> (Matthew 22:7)

Through this parable, Jesus declared to these leaders the certain destruction of their city and the end of their nation's covenantal relationship with God. They were being replaced with a "nation" producing the fruit of the Kingdom. Their city would burn!

As a result of this replacement the feast would go on, but the guest list would change. Jesus continued the parable:

> "The king said to his slaves, 'The wedding is ready, but
> those who were invited were not worthy. Go therefore
> to the main highways, and as many as you find there,
> invite to the wedding feast.'" (Matthew 22:8-9)

The invited guests, the people of Israel to whom belonged the promises made to the Patriarchs and the Prophets, would miss the wedding. Instead, a people who were not a people, another nation made up of the believing remnant of Israel and the believing Gentiles, would fill the banquet.

As that critical day of confrontation and debate continued, Jesus turned His attention more fully toward the leadership of the nation. With each progressive argument, the scribes and Pharisees heard the Lord's unrelenting statements of the certain destruction of their nation. His pronouncements of judgment reached a dramatic crescendo as Jesus delineated His litany of woes against the religious leadership of Israel. With each additional woe, the Lord built the case for their demise. The leaders who were to bring the nation into the Kingdom of God were themselves the greatest barricade. They were leading Israel to hell.

> "Woe to you scribes, Pharisees, hypocrites, because
> you shut off the kingdom of heaven from men; for
> you do not enter in yourselves, nor do you allow
> those who are entering to go in." (Matthew 23:13)

They had refused to receive the ministry of John the Baptist. John had come in fulfillment of the Prophets to gather the believing remnant and prepare the way for the coming of the Messiah. They had also refused to receive the ministry of the Lord Himself—the door into the Kingdom—in spite of the miraculous evidence and witness of God the Father that Jesus of Nazareth was the Christ. They were hypocrites! Under a disguise of righteousness, they hid polluted hearts. They had persuaded the nation that religious externalism was real piety and devotion to God. They prevented Israel from entering the Kingdom of God by their distorted interpretation of the Prophets, refusing to allow the hungry people to see Jesus in the Scripture.

> "Woe to you, scribes, Pharisees, hypocrites, because
> you devour widow's houses, even while for a pretense
> you make long prayers; therefore you shall receive
> greater condemnation." (Matthew 23:14)

All of their religious posturing could not hide the guilt of their actions. Their long prayers could not erase their greed. Women who had lost their husbands became their prey. They put on the appearance of extraordinary commitment and relationship to God that they might more easily take advantage of the widows! Yet, God had always defended the widows and instructed His people to provide for their welfare.

> "Woe to you, scribes, Pharisees, hypocrites, because
> you travel about on sea and land to make one con-
> vert; and when he becomes one, you make him twice
> the son of hell as yourself." (Matthew 23:15)

There was no overwhelming love of souls, no burning zeal for the honor of God in their making of converts. They were promoted only by carnal motives to make converts to their own opinions. And since they were on the way to hell, how could their converts be otherwise?

> "Woe to you, blind guides, who say, 'Whoever swears by the Temple, that is nothing; but whoever swears by the gold of the Temple, he is obligated.'" (Matthew 23:16)

They were the most important religious leaders of their day, yet they constantly used loop-holes to extricate themselves from vows and commitments they had made. Their unrighteous use of technicalities was an abomination to Jesus.

> "Woe to you, scribes, Pharisees, hypocrites! For you tithe the mint and dill and cumin, and have neglected the weightier provisions of the law; justice and mercy and faithfulness; but these are the things you should have done without neglecting the others." (Matthew 23:23)

These hypocrites were meticulous to extract every tiny tithe from the people. Yet they ministered without justice, mercy or faithfulness. The Lord was not censuring their attention to details, but was condemning their unwillingness to attend to the greater issues.

> "Woe to you, scribes, Pharisees, hypocrites! For you clean the outside of the cup and of the dish, but inside they are full of robbery and self-indulgence." (Matthew 23:25)

They were legally pure—outwardly perfect. Inwardly, they were sick! In their greed, they had robbed the people to fulfill their own appetites.

"Woe to you, scribes, Pharisees, hypocrites! For you are like whitewashed tombs which on the outside appear beautiful, but inside they are full of dead men's bones and all uncleanness." (Matthew 23:27)

Their religious shields which they had used to insure their positions of power were now useless against the Messiah who could see their hearts. Their hearts were at war with the God they supposedly served. They were full of death!

In His final woe the Lord exposes their hypocrisy in pretending to honor the Prophets while they were looking for a way in which to kill Him:

"Woe to you, Scribes and Pharisees, hypocrites! For you build the tombs of the prophets and adorn the monuments of the righteous, and say, 'If we had been living in the days of our fathers, we would not have been partners with them in shedding the blood of the prophets.'" (Matthew 23:29-30)

In *The Pulpit Commentary* Vol. 15, edited by H.D.M. Spence and Joseph F. Excell, one scholar observes:

"In the last [previous] woe Christ had spoken of sepulchers; he speaks of them here again, giving an unexpected view of the seeming honours paid to departed saints. The sumptuous mausoleums and tombs found e.g. round Jerusalem, and bearing the names of celebrated men (such as Zechariah, Absalom, Jehoshaphat), sufficiently attest the practice of the Jews in this matter. But the Pharisees' motives in acting thus were not pure; they were not influenced by respect for the prophets or repentance for national sins, but by pride, hypocrisy, and self-sufficiency." [10]

---

10 H. D. M. Spence and Joseph F. Excell eds., "Matthew," in The Pulpit Commentary Vol. 15, (Grand Rapids: Wm. B. Eerdmans, n.d.), p. 401.

Now, Jesus, looking into their hearts, and anticipating His own murder at their hands continued:

> "Woe to you, scribes, Pharisees, hypocrites!...you bear witness against yourselves, that you are sons of those who murdered the prophets. Fill up the measure of the guilt of your fathers. You serpents, you brood of vipers, how shall you escape the sentence of hell?" (Matthew 23:29-33)

As the sons of those who had murdered the Prophets, they would fill up the guilt of their fathers by crucifying the Lord of Glory and by persecuting the special messengers (apostles, prophets, evangelists, pastors, and teachers) that He would send to their particular generation following His resurrection, ascension, and the outpouring of the Holy Spirit. Their generation of Israelites would "kill and crucify" some of those who would be sent to them in the days immediately ahead, messengers of the Gospel of the Kingdom. Others they would "scourge" in their synagogues and "persecute from city to city." All of these things would happen in order that they might fill up "the measure of guilt" of their fathers and the judgment of God might come upon their nation and the city of Jerusalem for all the righteous blood of God's servants throughout the whole history of their nation.

Then Jesus added those awesome and terrible words which would provide the key to understanding the teaching He would give to His disciples on the Mount of Olives later that same day:

> "Truly I say to you, all these things shall come upon this generation." (Matthew 23:36)

Jesus was not speaking to some future generation—as some have insisted—but to the generation which was living at that time.

The Lord had come desiring to find the fruits of right-eousness and justice, yet instead He discovered sinful oppression throughout Israel. God had purposed Israel to be the light to the nations and the instrument of His Kingdom to teach the nations of the earth the righteousness of the Lord, which would result in filling the earth with justice. Yet, Israel had rebelled against God's will and refused to be the instrument of His purpose.

Ultimately, the rebellion of the nation would be complete.

The Prophets had promised the Messiah would come to a perverse generation of Jews and Israelites. At that time His righteous judgment would be poured out on the apostate nation. That day in the Temple court, as Jesus stood face to face with the religious leadership of the nation of Israel, He was facing the covenant-breaking generation of whom the Prophets had warned of coming judgment. This was the generation to which the Lord would direct the Olivet Discourse.

These were the most important leaders in all of Judaism. Jesus denounced them as hypocrites, blind guides, fools, whit-ed sepulchers, serpents, and a generation of vipers. Guilty! He accused them of shutting up the Kingdom of Heaven to the nation. Jesus accused them of extortion, of false teaching, and of lack of justice and faith. Their fate was sealed. They were the leaders of the generation the Prophets had predicted, the generation which would experience the judgment of God poured out upon the nation. Jesus spoke with a boldness belonging exclusively to the Son of God:

> "Fill up then the measure of the guilt of your fathers.
> You serpents, you brood of vipers, how shall you
> escape the sentence of hell." (Matthew 23:32)

Marcellus Kik, the great reformed theologian and scholar writes:

"The picture is that of a cup nearly filled and now
being filled to overflowing by the present [those living in the time of Christ and His disciples] generation of Jews. National sin, accumulated over many
centuries, had been trying the patience of God.
Again and again the Jews had sinned against their
God and forsaken him for idols. God had manifested
to them his forbearance and longsuffering and had
pleaded with the Jews to repent and return unto him.
Now, with the rejection of his Son and the crucifixion approaching, the patience of God had come to
an end. The cup of sin through this greatest of all
crimes would overflow and bring upon the nation
the terrible stroke of divine judgment." [11]

Jesus was declaring it was "this generation" which would
fill the cup to overflowing and experience the terrible wrath
of God:

"Therefore, behold, I am sending you prophets and
wise men and scribes; some of them you will kill and
crucify, and some of them you will scourge in your
synagogues, and persecute from city to city, that
upon you may fall the guilt of all the righteous blood
shed upon the earth..." (Matthew 23:34-35)

The Lord's words were direct: "that upon you," that particular specific generation, would fall the judgment for all
"the guilt of all the righteous blood ever shed" by the nation.
"Fill up then the measure of the guilt of your fathers." The
judgment would be a national judgment which would occur
during the generation to whom Jesus was speaking:

---

11 Marcellus Kik, An Eschatology of Victory, pp. 79-80.

"Truly I say unto you, all these things shall come upon this generation." (Matthew 23:36)

The rebellious nation would be judged. Jerusalem would soon be the target of the wrath of God.

Kik notes:

"…'This generation'…would fill the cup to overflowing and experience the terrible wrath of God." [12]

The city would be destroyed, and God's covenant with the Jewish nation would cease. With a broken heart Jesus cried with a loud voice so all might hear:

"O Jerusalem, Jerusalem, who kills the prophets and stones those who are sent to her! How often I wanted to gather your children together, the way a hen gathers her chicks under her wings, and you were unwilling." (Matthew 23:37)

With tears filling His Messianic eyes, Jesus warned the city with the most ominous prophecy of His ministry:

"Behold, your house is being left to you desolate!" (Matthew 23:38)

Kik adds:

"This was truly the sentence of death. God, as it were, forsook the Temple which had once been His dwelling place, and by His departure the Temple was left a sepulcher. It would henceforth be a blot upon the earth and fit only to be destroyed. Christ no longer called it 'my house' as He did in Matthew 21:13, but 'your house is left to you desolate.' The Temple thus was forsaken by the living God.

12 Kik, p. 80.

No longer would he dwell in the Holy of Holies of the earthly Temple. The House of God was now the House of Desolation. And being the House of Desolation its destruction was inevitable." [13]

Jesus said it clearly. Speaking each word with precision, He prophesied. Jerusalem and its Temple were about to be destroyed at the direction of heaven. Thus the setting for the Olivet Discourse.

---

13 Kik, p. 80.

2

THE SEARCH FOR THE SIGN

Jesus stunned Jerusalem with His prophecy:

"Behold, your house is being left to you desolate…"
(Matthew 23:38)

His words reverberated off every stone of the Temple. This was the single most important place in all of Judaism—the glory of every Jewish heart. Now, this Messiah, to whom the city had sung hosannas, had prophesied the destruction of the Temple and the city of Jerusalem. The implications of what He said were inconceivable. For the city to be destroyed, the seat of political power and the structure of the nation would be left in ruins. For the Temple to be desolate, the religious life of the nation would cease. The sacrifices would cease. The Levitical Priesthood would cease. Therefore, the age of Moses would cease. No Temple, no Old Covenant, no age of Moses would mean the culture of the nation would no longer exist.

Kik, commenting on the ramifications of Jesus' prophecy observes:

> "...the destruction of Jerusalem, which resulted in the excision of the Jewish nation from the Kingdom, was one of the most important events that has ever occurred on earth... it had tremendous consequences. The destruction of Jerusalem signalized that the old dispensation was over and was never to return." [1]

Hobbs writes:

> "...It involves the whole system of Judaism. God had sought repeatedly to use them, but to no avail. They had rejected the King, and now He fully and finally rejected them...Since they chose their way rather than His the King departed, leaving them to their own desires. These will finally result in the destruction of their temple, city, and nation. They themselves will be scattered. And their system of religion as they had known it will be no more. Their teachings will continue, but without the temple and the sacrifices. A people which were not a people will be called the people of God." [2]

Instantly, the atmosphere of the Temple dramatically changed. There were no more hosannas! Instead, cries of "Blasphemy!" began to fill the court. The nation knew exactly what Jesus was saying.

With one parting shot Jesus made an explicit declaration. Speaking as the Messiah, He declared:

---

[1] Kik, p. 75.

[2] Herschel H. Hobbs, <u>An Exposition of the Four Gospels: Volume 1 The Gospel of Matthew</u>, four volumes, (Nashville: Broadman, 1965), p. 330.

"For I say unto you, from now on you shall not see
Me until you say, 'Blessed is He who comes in the
name of the Lord!'" (Matthew 23:39)

Jesus drew upon the great Messianic Psalm of David [3] and claimed its title. He was Messiah! This was His day! The destruction of Jerusalem would prove it! Before their lives ended, these very Elders and Pharisees would see the Son of Man coming in the name of the Lord on the clouds of judgment. That judgment would declare to them in no uncertain terms the authenticity of His Messiahship.

The disciples were astounded. Hurriedly, they escorted Jesus out of the Temple. Perhaps wanting to change the subject, they pointed out the beauty of the Temple buildings. The magnificent structures rising hundreds of feet must have seemed absolutely impenetrable. Fifty years earlier Herod had designed and begun construction on these glorious edifices to rival and outlast the great pyramids of Egypt. The entire complex was the pride of Israel. However, the Lord was not deterred for a moment. Taking advantage of their fascination with the buildings He expanded His prophecy:

"Truly I say to you, not one stone here shall be left
upon another, which will not be torn down."
(Matthew 24:2)

Jerusalem would not only be destroyed, the Temple would be torn apart stone by stone. The disciples' generation would live to see it happen. It was by far the most powerful statement they had ever heard Jesus make. Obviously, they were overwhelmed by the thought of the destruction of their city and its magnificent Temple. Without saying a word they descended the winding road to the Kidron Valley and walked with Jesus up the steep ascent on the other side to the summit of the Mount of Olives. Struggling to understand, Peter, Andrew, James, and John came to Him privately and asked

---

3 Psalm 118.

Him two strategic questions which they had carried with them throughout the events of that incredible day: "when" and "what?" The search for the sign had begun.

The disciples' questions were extremely critical. They knew the ramifications of the Lord's prophetic declaration and could imagine its impact on their own lives and the lives of those in their generation. Their insightful questions involved three interrelated events: the destruction of the Temple, the coming of Jesus in power as Messiah and the end of the age in which they were living–the age of Moses. However, rather than asking three questions with three answers, they were actually searching for the timing of these events and the sign they were about to be fulfilled:

> "Tell us, when will these things be, and what will be the sign when all these things are going to be ful-filled?" (Mark 13:4)

Though the question of the timing of these events was far from being settled, the disciples certainly realized the coming of the Messianic Kingdom and the end of the Old Covenant era were related to the destruction of the city. Kik notes:

> "That their question relates to the destruction of the Temple is obvious from the context. They had just been pointing to the Temple and Jesus had declared concerning it, '…There shall not be left here one stone upon another that shall not be thrown down.' Immediately then the disciples ask, 'When shall these things be?' What could be more obvious than that the disciples are asking about the time when not one stone would remain upon another of the Temple." [4]

---

[4] Kik, p. 85.

Jesus was speaking to them, of their concerns, not to some future generation of Jews. If He was telling them of events which had no significance to their lives, He would have clearly told them so. But He did not. Rather, Jesus spoke directly to them and answered their insightful question. Whatever confusion the disciples had concerning the timing or the nature of the Kingdom, they certainly understood that Jesus was speaking of the destruction of the Temple and relating its destruction to the coming of His Kingdom and the end of the age of Moses–the age in which they were living.

This was *not* the first time the disciples had heard these things–THEY HAD HEARD THE SONG OF MOSES.

The Old Testament Prophets had promised such a devastation coinciding with the establishing of Messiah's Kingdom. A constant theme running throughout the Old Testament Prophets was the judgment of the nation for her rebellion and the insistence that the end of the covenant of Moses would be ushered in by the destruction of Jerusalem. In fact, Moses himself had prophesied that the end of the Old Covenant age and the dawning of Messiah's Day would come with the destruction of the nation:

> "Assemble before me all the elders of your tribes and all your officials so that I can speak these words in their hearing and call heaven and earth to testify against them. For I know that after my death you are sure to become utterly corrupt and to turn from the way I have commanded you; and evil will befall you in *the latter days*, for you will do that which is evil in the sight of the Lord, provoking Him to anger with the works of your hands. Then Moses spoke in the hearing of all the assembly of Israel the words of this song…" (Deuteronomy 31:28-30)

The disciples were like any other devout Jews. They knew Moses had prophesied a generation which would be so corrupt the judgment of God would ultimately come against them with disaster. This would mean their removal as the covenantal people, the end of the sacrificial system and the end of the age of Moses. Remarkably, Moses prophesied the end of the Old Covenant people. They would no longer be the children of God:

> "They have acted corruptly toward Him. To their shame they are no longer His children, but a warped and crooked generation." (Deuteronomy 32:5)

Moses had seen a generation of Israel which would be so corrupt and rebellious against the Lord that their lives would demand the judgment of God:

> "…I will hide my face from them, I will see *what their end will be*; for they are a perverse generation, sons in whom is no faithfulness." (Deuteronomy 32:20)

Moses thus envisioned and prophesied the end of the Old Covenant people of God.

Only a few weeks after Jesus gave His Olivet Discourse, the Apostle Peter stood and preached to his generation of Jews to:

> "Be saved from this perverse generation." (Acts 2:40)

It was obvious Peter believed the generation about which Moses was singing was the generation to whom Peter was preaching on the day of Pentecost.

The disciples knew this prophetic song of Moses. They also knew Moses was not singing about the people he led out of Egypt. They knew He was singing a song about a future generation of Jews which would experience the end of the Old

Covenant era and the dawning of Messiah's day. Their searching question was to know if He was singing about the generation in which they were living.

The song of Moses would answer their question:

> "But Jeshurun grew fat and wicked...He abandoned the God who made him...They made him jealous with their foreign gods and angered him with their detestable idols. The Lord saw this and rejected them...for they are a perverse generation, children who are unfaithful. They made me jealous by what is no god and angered me with their worthless idols." (Deuteronomy 32:15-21) (NIV)

Moses then made an extraordinary statement. It was a statement which sent a chill down the spine of every Jew. It spelled the end of their national covenantal relationship with God.

> "I will make them envious by those who are not a people...I will make them angry by a nation that has no understanding." (Deuteronomy 32:21)

Moses was forecasting the Church! He looked forward thousands of years into the future and saw the New Covenant people of God. He predicted the new Israel made up of believing Jews and Gentiles. Later in his apostolic ministry, Peter specifically identified the Church as this people who were not a nation:

> "But you are a chosen race, a royal priesthood, a holy nation...for you were once not a people, but now you are the people of God." (1 Pet. 2:9-10)

But on this day, Peter's mind had to be spinning. Was his day that day prophesied by Moses—the day when God would

LIBRARY
WILLOW MEADOWS BAPTIST CHURCH
9999 GREENWILLOW
HOUSTON, TEXAS 77035

pour out His wrath? He knew full well that time would be filled with fire and destruction, for it was the content of the song Moses sang:

> "For a fire has been kindled by my wrath...one that
> burns to the realm of death below...it will devour
> the earth and its harvest and set afire the foundations
> of the mountains." (Deuteronomy 32:22)

> "For they are a nation without sense, there is no dis-
> cernment." (Deuteronomy 32:28)

The disciples kept remembering Moses' prophetic song. They had heard Moses read again and again in the Temple. Against the backdrop of the song of Moses the disciples were asking Jesus on the Mount of Olives:

> "When will these things happen, what will be the
> sign of your coming and of the end of the age?"
> (Matthew 24:3)

The disciples were not asking about the end of the world or the physical universe. They were not asking about the end of some future generation nor the end of an age thousands of years removed from their own day; they were asking about the end of the age in which they were living. Kik observes:

> "There is no doubt the disciples believed that the
> destruction of the Temple and the end of the age
> were one and the same thing." [5]

As they questioned the Lord Jesus, they remembered more:

> "Have I not kept this in reserve?"
> (Deuteronomy 32:34)

---

[5] Kik, p. 88.

Moses was singing about something happening at the end of his age. It would be a day of vengeance which would spell doom upon the apostate nation:

> "And sealed it in my vaults, it is mine to avenge…I will repay…in due time their foot will slip, their day of disaster is near. Their doom rushes upon them." (Deuteronomy 32:34-35)

Jehovah was swearing an oath through Moses:

> "I lift my hand to heaven and declare as surely as I live forever when I sharpen my flashing sword and my hand grasps it in judgment I will take vengeance on my adversaries and repay those who hate me." (Deuteronomy 32:40-41)

> "Rejoice, O nations, with His people; for He will avenge the blood of His servants, He will take vengeance on His enemies and make atonement for His land and people." (Deuteronomy 32:43)

Luke recorded Jesus as identifying this time of vengeance as the destruction of Jerusalem in A.D. 70:

> "When you see Jerusalem surrounded by armies, then recognize that her desolation is at hand…these are days of vengeance, in order that all things which are written may be fulfilled." (Luke 21:20-22)

What an incredible song! Moses, the mediator of the Old Covenant to the nation of Israel, sang a song to his own people prophesying the ultimate destruction of his nation because of its people's rebellion against the God who had loved them and called them to be His own. Every Jew knew Moses. Every disciple knew Moses. Their searching questions centered on the matter of timing—when would this take place, and what would be the sign they were about to happen?

THEY HAD HEARD ISAIAH AND
THE SONG OF THE LAMB.

Moses was not the only prophetic voice which had sounded the alarm of the judgment and the wrath of God. Having been raised in the Jewish synagogues, the disciples of Jesus were all very familiar with the great Prophets—especially Isaiah. They knew well this Prophet had seen a Jerusalem worthy of being destroyed by the judgment of God:

"See how the faithful city has become a harlot! She once was full of justice; righteousness used to dwell in her, but now murderers! Your silver has become dross, your choice wine is diluted with water. Your rulers are rebels, companions of thieves, they all love bribes and chase after gifts. They do not defend the cause of the fatherless…the widow's case does not come before them." (Isaiah 1:21-23)

Jerusalem a harlot!

Isaiah had joined with Moses in seeing a Jerusalem which would be filled with injustice and unrighteousness, a city rebelling against the covenant of God. This was the reason Jesus denounced the Pharisees, scribes, and religious leaders of Israel. The disciples had been standing at His side as He condemned the religious leadership of Israel for its rebellion. Righteous judgment did not exist. Justice did not exist. Because of its lawlessness, Isaiah had promised catastrophic judgment would come upon Israel. Isaiah had timed this judgment with the resurrection of Messiah:

"Men will flee to the caves and the rocks and to holes in the ground from the dread of the Lord and the splendor of His majesty when He rises to shake the earth." (Isaiah 2:19)

These awesome prophetic words had to be ringing in the minds of the disciples as the pieces of their Messianic puzzle began to take shape. This was why Jesus had so clearly spoken of His death and resurrection. The victorious resurrection of the Messiah was a major theme for the Old Testament Prophets:

"When He rises to shake the earth.
The Lord arises to contend,
And stands to judge the people.
The Lord enters into judgment with the elders and
princes of His people,
'It is you who have devoured the vineyard;
The plunder of the poor is in your houses.
What do you mean by crushing My people,
And grinding the face of the poor?'
Declares the Lord God of hosts." (Isaiah 3:13-15)

Isaiah was prophesying the resurrection of Messiah and its ramifications. It was the resurrected Messiah who would destroy the nation and bring an end to the age of Moses. That much was clear to the disciples. Their questions followed that understanding. What would be the sign of the coming destruction of Jerusalem?

As the disciples searched for an answer, the words of Isaiah must have echoed in their memories:

"In that day the branch of the Lord will be beautiful
and glorious, and the fruit of the land will be the
pride and glory of the survivors in Israel. Those who
are left in Zion who remain in Jerusalem, will be
called holy, all who are recorded among the living in
Jerusalem." (Isaiah 4:2)

Something would take place in Jerusalem so convulsive that only a remnant would survive. Isaiah saw the remnant as holy. The Prophet predicted a believing remnant which would still be standing when the fire of Messiah's judgment fell upon the city:

> "The Lord will wash away the filth of the women of Zion, He will cleanse the blood stains from Jerusalem by a spirit of judgment and a spirit of fire." (Isaiah 4:4)

This was Isaiah's reference to the fire of Messiah's judgment. Earlier in the Lord's ministry, Jesus used the Prophet's words to speak of His bringing the judgment of fire:

> "I came to cast fire on the earth, and how I wish it were already kindled! But I have a baptism to undergo." (Luke 12:49-50)

Jesus constantly incorporated the prophetic passages of Isaiah into His preaching, teaching, and parables. He had trained His disciples on the words of the Prophets.

Isaiah prophetically envisioned the Servant of Jehovah, the Son of God, singing a song for His Father concerning His vineyard:

> "I will sing for the one I love, a song about his vineyard." (Isaiah 5:1)

In Isaiah 53, the Prophet declared that this servant would suffer and die as a lamb to make atonement for sin. In the fullness of time, John the Baptist introduced the Lord Jesus as the Lamb of God who would take away the sins of the world. Because of this and Christ's sacrificial death on the Cross, the song of Isaiah's suffering servant came to be known in the early Church as the Song of the Lamb (Revelation 15:3). This Song of the Lamb, like the song Moses sang, forecasted the destruction of Jerusalem:

"My loved one had a vineyard on a fertile hillside.
He dug it up and cleared it of stones and planted it
with the choicest vines. He built a watchtower in it
and cut out a winepress as well, then he looked for a
crop of good grapes, but it yielded only bad fruit.
Now you dwellers in Jerusalem and men of Judah
judge between me and my vineyard." (Isaiah 5:2-3)

Earlier, during that last week of His life, as Jesus taught in
the Temple, the disciples had heard Him use this passage in
His own vineyard parable. He had spoken of the "son of the
vineyard owner" who was killed by the wicked tenants, the
same Lamb of God who would die for the sin of a wicked
world:

"Listen to another parable, there was a landowner
who planted a vineyard. He put a wall around it and
dug a winepress in it and built a watchtower."
(Matthew 21:33)

These were critically important words to the disciples. They
knew Isaiah. Jesus continued:

"Then he rented the vineyard to some farmers and
went away on a journey. When the harvest time
approached he sent his servants to the tenants to col-
lect his fruit. The tenants seized his servants; they
beat one, killed another, and stoned a third. Then he
sent other servants to them the same way. Last of all,
he sent his son to them. They will respect my son he
said. But when the tenants saw the son they said to
each other, 'This is the heir. Come, let's kill him and
take his inheritance.' So they took him, threw him
out of the vineyard and killed him. Therefore when
the owner of the vineyard comes what will he do to
those tenants?" (Matthew 21:33-40)

There was nothing coincidental when Jesus used Isaiah 5 as the basis for His parable. In fact, Isaiah's song of the servant and the vineyard parable of Jesus both were at the heart of the Lord's Olivet Discourse. Both were speaking of the destruction of Jerusalem by the Lord:

"He would bring those wretches to a wretched end." (Matthew 21:41)

The timing of the wretched end of Jerusalem was at the heart of the disciples' questions. They were not questioning the timing for the end of the world, but the prophesied wretched end of Jerusalem. The Lord continued the parable:

"...and will rent the vineyard to other tenants, who will give him his share of the crop at harvest time. Jesus said to them, 'Have you never read in the scriptures: The stone the builders rejected has become the capstone. The Lord has done this, and it is marvelous in our eyes.'" (Matthew 21:41-42)

Then Jesus made an incredibly poignant statement:

"Therefore, I tell you the kingdom of God will be taken away from you, and be given to a nation producing the fruit of it." (Matthew 21:43)

Exactly as the song of Moses stated! Exactly as Isaiah prophesied! The Kingdom would be given to a nation producing the fruit of the Kingdom.

"Now I will tell you what I'm going to do to my vineyard, I will take away its hedge, and it will be destroyed. I will break down its wall, and it will be trampled. I will make it a wasteland, neither pruned nor cultivated.

"The vineyard of the Lord Almighty is the house of
Israel, and the men of Judah are the garden of His
delight. And He looked for justice but saw bloodshed; for righteousness, but heard cries of distress."
(Isaiah 5:5-7)

What an exciting moment this had to be for the disciples.
For three years they had been with the Lord. Now, the most
important teachings and promises Jesus had made concerning
His Kingdom were coming into focus. The Prophets' promises were about to be fulfilled by His death on the cross, His
resurrection from the dead, His ascension to the Father, His
pouring out of the Spirit, and His judgment of fire. By His
suffering and death, Jesus would accomplish redemption for
the believing Jewish remnant and the multitude of Gentiles
who would believe in Him, and He would bring judgment
upon those who rejected Him as Messiah:

"He who falls on this stone will be broken to pieces;
but on whomever it falls, it will scatter like dust."
(Matthew 21:44)

This was not good news to everyone standing in the
Temple that day. The Chief Priests and Pharisees knew Jesus
was targeting them with His rebukes:

"When the Chief Priests and the Pharisees heard
Jesus' parables, they understood that He was speaking
about them." (Matthew 21:44-45)

They were the responsible men, the leaders of the nation,
who were supposed to lead the nation into righteousness. But
they had not done so! There was no fruit of the Kingdom in
Jerusalem—no justice! Isaiah had prophesied it, and John the
Baptist had railed against it. Now, Jesus was standing before
them claiming to be the Messiah and denouncing the reli-

gious leadership of Israel for the lack of justice in the nation.

Justice would be the essence of Messiah's Kingdom as the Old Testament prophets had promised. The Kingdom would be taken from the unfruitful nation of Israel. The Lord would raise up regenerated men and women to form a New Holy Nation, the Church, which would bring forth the fruit of the Kingdom–righteousness, peace, and joy in the whole earth. The Lord would work with this New Israel from the right hand of Majesty on High, executing righteous judgment upon men and nations upon the basis of their response to the Gospel of the Kingdom of God. The hallmark of Messiah's Kingdom would be the filling of the entire earth with justice! Messianic judgment would be certain.

The disciples had not only heard the prophetic words of Moses and Isaiah–THEY HAD HEARD THE BAPTIST.

The disciples of Jesus knew John the Baptist. Most of them had been his disciples first. They knew without question he was a Prophet, a man of no compromise, and a messenger sent from God. They were there in the wilderness when his giant voice cried out to the nation:

"Repent, for the kingdom of heaven is at hand."
(Matthew 3:2)

Choosing the company of the Baptist to announce His Son was divinely deliberate. John had been selected from the dawn of creation to be the Voice who would trumpet Messiah's arrival. The prophet Isaiah had pledged a forerunner who would prepare the way for the promised Son of God:

"A voice is calling, 'Clear the way for the Lord in the wilderness; make smooth in the desert a highway for our God.'" (Isaiah 40:3)

John was the great time-man sent by God to alert the nation that the time for the fulfillment of all their hopes and dreams concerning the Kingdom of Messiah had arrived.

Not only was the Baptist the forerunner announcing the presence of Messiah, John had also preceded Jesus with his message of national desolation, calling for repentance. Contrary to the Jewish peoples' desire for a political offer of a restored Jewish Kingdom, the Baptist was breathing the fire of immediate judgment. His had not been a positive message assuring the nation of its freedom from Rome. Indeed, his message was replete with the words of judgment from the great Old Testament prophets. John had recognized Jesus as the promised Son of David and had seen in Him the fulfillment of Isaiah's prophecy proclaiming the certain destruction of Old Covenant Israel and the dawning of Messiah's new Kingdom.

John did not believe Messiah was coming to offer the Jews a restored national Kingdom. Instead, the Baptist demanded that Jesus had come to destroy the apostate nation and establish the new Israel of God. From the opening of his prophetic declaration, John the Baptist was in concert with Isaiah. They both saw the coming Son of God who would take His vengeance upon the rebellious nation:

"Alas, sinful nation,
People weighed down with iniquity,
Offspring of evildoers,
Sons who act corruptly!
They have abandoned the Lord,
They have despised the Holy One of Israel,
They have turned away from Him…
The whole head is sick,
The whole heart is faint…
Your land is desolate,

Your cities are burned with fire...
It is desolation, as overthrown by strangers."
(Isaiah 1:4-7)

It was Isaiah in this same passage who, looking ahead to the baptism ministry of John, demanded the nation be washed as preparation for the coming Son of David:

"Wash yourselves, make yourselves clean;
Remove the evil of your deeds from My sight...
If you consent and obey,
You will eat the best of the land;
But if you refuse and rebel,
You will be devoured by the sword." (Isaiah 1:16-19)

The Baptist stood in the wilderness and cried out to the apostate nation regarding their sin and need of repentance. Identifying them in their rebellion as children of Satan, he warned them of falsely relying upon Abraham as their security:

"You brood of vipers, who warned you to flee from the wrath to come? Therefore bring forth fruits in keeping with repentance, and do not say to your-selves, 'We have Abraham as our father,' for I say to you that God is able from these stones to raise up children to Abraham." (Luke 3:7-8)

To the Jews of John's day, Abraham was their salvation. They believed that every blessing they enjoyed came directly from their blood relationship with the patriarch. Edersheim explains:

"For, no principle was more fully established in the popular conviction, than that all Israel had part in the world to come...and this, specifically, because of their connection with Abraham...In fact, by their descent from Abraham, all the children of Israel were nobles, infinitely higher than any proselytes...the ships on the sea were preserved through the merit of Abraham; the rain descended on account of it...his righteousness had on many occasions been the support of Israel's cause...his merit availed even for the wicked. In its extravagance the Midrash thus apostrophises Abraham: 'If thy children were even (morally) dead bodies, without blood vessels or bones, thy merit would avail for them!'" [6]

Nonetheless, the unthinkable was happening. Multitudes were going to the wilderness to be baptized by John—Jews were being baptized! No Prophet ever baptized a Jew. Only the Gentile converts needed to be "washed." Now, the forerunner of the Messiah was calling the believing remnant out of the old nation—which was headed for destruction—into the new Holy Nation which the Messiah would establish upon the foundation of the New Covenant in His blood. They were to enter into the new Messianic Kingdom, for the old Mosaic Kingdom was doomed by the Prophets. By submitting themselves to John's baptism, they were acknowledging their defilement; they were seeking purification and admission into the New Holy Nation of Messiah.

In his great work, *New Testament Theology*, Frank Stagg, the highly respected Baptist theologian, speaks of the uniqueness of John's baptism of Jewish converts as the calling of the remnant out of apostate Israel:

"The major innovation of John's baptism, however, was in the calling of Jews to repentance baptism. Proselyte baptism was for Gentiles; John baptized Jews. To John the Jews were alien to true Israel or the

---

[6] Alfred Edersheim, The Life and Times of Jesus the Messiah, 2 vols. in one, (1994; 2nd reprint ed., Peabody, MA: Hendrickson, 1993), pp. 188, see also, The Midrash (or Commentary) Bereshith Rabba, on Genesis.

people of Messiah...John's repentance baptism marked a Jew's incorporation into the community awaiting the Kingdom of God. John's baptism was basically eschatological; it looked toward the coming of Messiah to establish the Kingdom of God...

He refused baptism to many because they had not shown evidences of repentance (Matthew 3:8, Luke 3:3)...He called for confession of sins (Mark 1:5) and social righteousness (Luke 3:10-14) as evidence of a radical change in one's way of life. John was not preaching reform; he was proclaiming the coming of the Lord (Kurios), who would "baptize with the Holy Spirit and fire" (Matthew 3:11, Luke 3:16)." [7]

With his message of certain national disaster, the Baptist continued to gather the believing remnant of Israel by calling for repentance, baptizing those who came and declaring:

"Repent, repent the kingdom of God is at hand!"

The Kingdom of God was breaking in on them. John was demanding they "flee the wrath to come." There was no word of national restoration! Indeed, the message was one of national destruction at the hand of the coming Son of David, the Messiah; who reigning as King of Kings would bring salvation to His flock, the believing remnant, and baptize the rebels with the judgment of fire from the throne of His father David in heaven. The great forerunner, the voice in the wilderness, was crying out to the apostate nation to prepare for the coming of the Son of God, the ruling shepherd who was bringing the Spirit and fire to inaugurate the new and destroy the old.

John purposely positioned himself in the wilderness. It was there Isaiah had promised the new Kingdom would

---

[7] Frank Stagg, New Testament Theology, (Nashville: Broadman, 1962), pp. 212-213.

begin. It was there, at the Baptism of the Son of David, the new rivers of the Spirit would be opened up for those who would have ears to hear and hearts to believe. John took his stand outside the city to call for the believing remnant to separate themselves, to come out of the apostasy of their wicked generation and to come into the newness of the Lord's Day:

"Do not call to mind the former things,
Or ponder the things of the past.
Behold, I will do something new,
Now it will spring forth;
Will you not be aware of it?
I will even make a roadway in the wilderness,
Rivers in the desert." (Isaiah 43:18-19)

Into this setting of national conviction and rebuke walked the Son of God to be baptized by John, fulfilling the prophecies of the Son of David. He did not come to change the message of John, but to reinforce it and identify with it. Foreshadowing His own death, burial and resurrection, and anticipating the outpouring of the Holy Spirit upon the believing remnant of Israel and the Gentile nations, Jesus openly submitted to baptism, gladly identifying with the mission of the Son of David to bring "justice to the nations":

"Behold my servant, whom I uphold; my chosen one in whom my soul delights. I have put my Spirit upon Him; He will bring forth justice to the nations" (Isaiah 42:1).

The Baptist had alerted his followers to this coming one by boldly stating:

"As for me I baptize you with water; but One is coming who is mightier than I, and I am not fit to untie the thongs of His sandals; He will baptize you with

the Holy Spirit and fire. And His winnowing fork is
in His hand to thoroughly clear His threshing floor,
and to gather the wheat into His barn; but He will
burn up the chaff with unquenchable fire."
(Luke 3:16-17)

The One coming after John would not only baptize with
"the Holy Spirit," speaking of the regenerating and empower-
ing work of the Spirit of God, but also with "fire," speaking of
the judgment of God. According to John, God's anointed
King would not only pour out the renewing power of the
Spirit but also the purging power of the fire of judgment
throughout history, beginning with that first century generation of Jews. John thundered that all men and nations would
be baptized by the Messiah, either with the Spirit and power
of God or by His judgment and wrath. John the Baptist
announced a Messiah who would baptize the nation of Israel
with the Holy Spirit and fire. There was no offer of a political
restoration. He would not be that kind of Messiah. The
Baptist knew the prophetic dimensions of the Messiah. He
could quote by heart the proclamations of Isaiah, declaring
the good news that the Son of God would come to gather the
believing remnant:

"Behold, the Lord God will come with might,
With His arm ruling for Him.
Behold, His reward is with Him,
And His recompense before Him.
Like a shepherd He will tend His flock,
In His arms He will gather His lambs,
And carry them in His bosom;
He will gently lead the nursing ewes."
(Isaiah 40:10-11)

Simultaneously, John was aware of the dual baptism of
Messiah. The prophets from Moses to Malachi had promised

the day of Messiah's judgment, when He would throw fire upon the earth to avenge His enemies:

"For behold, the Lord will come in fire
and His chariots like the whirlwind,
to render His anger with fury,
and His rebuke with flames of fire." (Isaiah 66:15)

Israel was both intrigued and fearful of the Baptist. Thousands went to the wilderness to hear this Prophet. Repenting of their sins, hundreds of Jews were baptized into the believing remnant, which would ultimately pass safely through the great tribulation and be joined with believing Gentiles to comprise the Church, the new Israel. They would live through the transitional generation, which would see New Covenant Israel established before Old Covenant Israel would be destroyed. John the Baptist was the promised Elijah who would call the believing remnant out of the perverse generation in preparation for the formation of the new creation, the Church, the new Israel of God.

Earlier in the Lord's ministry, His disciples had asked Jesus a direct question regarding this coming Elijah:

"Why do the scribes say that Elijah must come first?
And He answered and said, 'Elijah is coming and will
restore all things; but I say unto you, that Elijah
already came, and they did not recognize him, but
did whatever they wished. So also the Son of Man is
going to suffer at their hands.' The disciples understood that He had spoken to them about John the
Baptist." (Matthew 17:10-13)

The Lord's answer to the disciples had been precise. The Baptist had indeed been the forerunner, the great time-man who marked the end of the old age and the dawning of the new. He appeared as the prophetic man and prepared the way for the Lord and His judgment. The judgment which had been prophesied by Moses, Isaiah, Malachi and others was coming upon that perverse generation. But before the fire of Messiah's judgment would be poured out upon the apostates, the Lord would first gather the remnant and seal them with the Holy Spirit of promise. The New Covenant people of God would then become the instrument of Messiah's Kingdom through which the nations of the earth would be disciplined and God's saving rule would be established in the earth.

Their time with John the Baptist had prepared the disciples for the Olivet Discourse. The wrath of God was coming. It was about to be poured out upon their apostate nation. The disciples knew of John's warning of coming wrath. Critical in their understanding of the Olivet Discourse was their realization that Jesus was not prophesying His second coming at the end of the world, but the ramifications of His first coming, which involved His judgment upon their generation, the last generation of the age of Moses.

THEY HAD HEARD JESUS.

Jesus' prophecy in the Temple complex was not the first time His disciples had heard Him speak of the end of the age, or His Messianic coming in judgment. Some of their most important times with the Lord were after the crowds would leave and they would have Him alone. On one particular occasion, the crowds had been very large and questions from the scribes and Pharisees very pointed. Ultimately, He turned from the demands of the multitude and taught the twelve. Jesus took His disciples through a litany of topics when He abruptly changed the direction of His teaching and made an incredible statement. The change had to catch the disciples off guard:

"I have come to bring fire on the earth!"

He continued:

"How I wish it were already kindled!" (Luke 12:49)

They knew the Old Testament prophetic analogy of fire. Fire meant judgment! The impact of His statement had to be powerful. They realized again who He actually was. They were standing in the presence of the "Fire Messiah" who would ultimately release the judgment of God upon the apostate nation—just as the prophets had predicted.

Remembering these special private moments with Jesus made their search for an answer on the Mount of Olives even more important. When would this fire fall? What would be the sign?

They had also heard Him speak warnings to Jerusalem. Just hours before He gave His Olivet Discourse, He predicted the coming doom of Jerusalem:

"As He approached Jerusalem and saw the city He wept over it and said, 'If you, even you, had only known on this day what would bring you peace but now it is hidden from your eyes. The days will come upon you when your enemies will build an embankment against you and encircle you and hem you in on every side. They will dash you to the ground, you and the children within your walls. They will not leave one stone on another.'" (Luke 19:41-44)

He prepared the disciples for the prophecy He would deliver in the Temple. They were fully aware of the prophets' demands of destruction, and they knew Jesus was to fulfill those prophecies. They understood all these things would take place during their lives, their generation. Nonetheless, they were searching for the sign of the prophetic fulfillment.

There was another moment perhaps even more powerful. Jesus was alone with His disciples when He shared with them the details of His Messianic mission. He was never more direct:

> "Jesus Christ began to show His disciples that He
> must go to Jerusalem, and suffer many things from
> the elders and Chief Priests and scribes, and be
> killed, and be raised up on the third day."
> (Matthew 16:21)

Peter would not hear of such a thing. He took Jesus aside and rebuked Him:

> "God forbid it, Lord! This will never happen to you."
> (Matthew 16:22)

Jesus turned to Peter:

> "Get behind Me, Satan! You are a stumbling block to
> Me; for you are not setting your mind on God's
> interest, but man's." (Matthew 16:23)

Peter's interest was Jesus. The Lord's interest was the will of God. Everything God had planned from the dawn of creation was about to be completed. Jesus was facing the cross, recognizing its part in the eternal plan. It would be the means by which He would destroy the power of the kingdom of darkness and accomplish the redemption of the world. Through His death and resurrection, He would crush the head of the serpent, remit sins, destroy death, and set the captives free. The cross would be the door through which He would ascend back to the Father and receive His Kingdom.

As John would write in His Gospel, the cross was the moment of His glorification. As King of Kings, Jesus would "come in His Father's glory" and bring judgment upon the apostate nation. Some of these very disciples would be alive when it happened.

> "For the Son of Man is going to come in His Father's glory with His angels and then He will reward each person according to what he's done. I tell you the truth, some who are standing here will not taste death before they see the Son of Man coming in his kingdom…" (Matthew 16:27)

Who was standing there? Peter, Andrew, James, John—the *same ones* who came to Him on the Mount of Olives *searching* for the sign of the Kingdom. They were the specific ones to whom Jesus had directly said, "You will not taste of death before you see the Son of Man coming in His Kingdom." He was speaking to them—His disciples. This had to be over-whelming news. Some of them would not die before His coming in power and glory. They would live to see His Kingdom. These were the same men He had previously told:

> "To you it has been granted to know the mysteries of the kingdom…" (Matthew 13:11)

> "For truly I say to you, that many prophets and right-eous men desired to see what you see, and did not see it; and to hear what you hear, and did not hear it." (Matthew 13:17)

Moses had prepared them. Isaiah had challenged them. The Baptist had warned them. Jesus Himself had told them they would see the Kingdom.

As Peter, James, John and Andrew approached Him that evening on the Mount of Olives, their minds had to be rac-ing. Looking across the Kidron valley below and beholding the majestic splendor of the Temple and of their beloved city, they processed the events of that day and heard His prophet-ic words echoing in their ears:

"O Jerusalem, Jerusalem... Behold your house is left unto you desolate!" (Matthew 23:37-38)

"Truly, I say unto you, not one stone here shall be left upon another, which will not be torn down." (Matthew 24:2)

The questions rose up out of their spirits! With searching questions they boldly asked the Lord Jesus, when will these things happen and what will be the sign of the Kingdom?

3

THE SPURIOUS SIGNS

Late in the afternoon, Jesus left the Temple for the last time. Walking through Solomon's Porch with its covered colonnade, He and His twelve exited the city through the Eastern Gate. They crossed the shadow filled Kidron Valley, and climbed the curving road up the Mount of Olives. At every turn, the city was in their view. Jerusalem at that time of day was alive with colors as the setting sun bathed its massive marble walls and tiny terraced courts with a heavenly mixture of golds and reds. Rising majestically over one hundred feet above the city were the glittering golden spikes on the roof of the Temple. As evening continued, the sun slowly disappearing directly behind Jerusalem, the grandeur, the symmetry and the radiant sheen of snowy marble and gold certainly stood out gloriously. The sun had cast the shadow of the city's gigantic walls across the darkened valley and up the slope of the Mount of Olives. From the disciples' perspective, Jerusalem must have seemed so impenetrable that nothing could ever destroy it. Much less could they imagine their magnificent Temple torn apart stone by stone. Yet, they had clearly heard the words of Jesus:

> "Not one stone here left on top of another that will
> not be torn down." (Matthew 24:2)

One after the other commented about the city. Pointing out the massive stones–some nearly twenty-five feet long–they repeatedly called His attention to the sacred capitol. In silence Jesus continued up the mountain. Reaching the summit, He paused. The entire city was then laid out before them. The thoughts which had to be fomenting in the minds of the disciples were unimaginable. At some moment, standing on that great vista, Peter, James, John and Andrew finally approached the Lord for clarification:

> "Tell us, when will these things be, and what will be
> the sign of your coming and the end of the age?"
> (Matthew 24:3)

It was a critical moment for Jesus and His disciples. Christianity was about to be inaugurated on the strength of their lives. They had to understand–clearly understand–what Jesus was saying.

Jesus responded:

> "See to it that no one misleads you..."
> (Matthew 24:4)

What a remarkable way to respond to their question. Rather than answering outright, Jesus began His explanation with a warning. It was a directed warning–directed to four specific disciples, Peter, James, John and Andrew. It was a warning concerning events that would characterize the last days of the Old Covenant era, the period lasting from A.D. 30 to A.D. 70.

This period just before the end of the age of Moses would be characterized by events which could be misleading, even deceiving to these first disciples. The great Baptist scholar John A. Broadus quotes Alexander in his commentary on what he calls "misleading signs:"

"The divine wisdom of the Saviour and his knowledge of the perils which beset his followers are strikingly exemplified in this preliminary warning against error and delusion, this exposure of false signs before giving a description of the true."[1]

Jesus was surrounded by the future leaders of His Church. It was critical to their success that they not be misled. So, the Lord clearly warned them about certain misleading or false signs. His warning was directed to them and their lifetime.

In *Last Days Madness* Gary DeMar correctly observes:

"Notice that the warning was addressed to Jesus' disciples: 'See that no one misleads *you*.' They would be hearing of 'wars and rumors of wars.' Jesus said, 'See that *you* are not frightened.' The disciples would be delivered up to tribulation: 'They will kill *you*,' and '*you* will be hated.' The conclusion is obvious: Jesus' warning was to the generation of disciples who asked the question about the Temple and who heard His response." [emphasis in original] [2]

Knowing the ordeal these men would face as they led the infant Church, Jesus cautioned them not to be misled by false signs of the Kingdom.

DeMar concludes:

---

[1] J. Addison Alexander, cited in John A. Broadus, Commentary on the Gospel of Matthew, ed. Alva Hovey, (Philadelphia: American Baptist Publication Society, 1886), pp. 482-483.
[2] Gary DeMar, Last Days Madness: Obsession of the Modern Church, (Atlanta: American Vision, 1994), p. 60.

"The conclusion is obvious: Jesus' warning was to the generation of disciples who asked the question about the Temple and who heard His response."[3]

The conclusion is "obvious," that is, to anyone whose mind is truly open to the reality of the situation. It is important to remember, Jesus was answering their questions—not ours! They had specifically asked, "Tell *us*, when will these things be...," speaking of the destruction of Jerusalem and the Temple which lay before them. They were not asking about a future, restored Temple to be built by a future generation of Israelites but the Temple they had just exited and about which Jesus had only moments before declared, "Do *you* not see all these things?...not one stone here shall be left upon another..." He was speaking of the immediate Temple in their day, not some distant future one. He was answering their question introduced by the words "Tell *us*..." They had been very specific! As Jesus answered, He also was very specific, "See to it that no one misleads *you*..." Throughout this discourse, the Lord uses the second person plural pronoun "you," indicating He was speaking to these disciples and not to some future generation of disciples.

Therefore Jesus warned these disciples. He spoke directly to Peter, James, John, Andrew and the others. They were about to lead the Church through some of its most perilous times. They must not be misled. They must know what they were facing. Therefore, the Lord gave them a detailed list of misleading or false signs:

Misleading Sign # 1
False Messiahs

"Jesus answered and said to them, 'See that no one mislead you. For many will come in My name, saying, 'I am the Christ,' and will mislead many.'"
(Matthew 24:4-5)

3 DeMar, p. 60.

The generation in which Jesus and His disciples lived was
a time for "messiahs." Jews knew the prophecies of Daniel.
They knew Daniel had, through his interpretation of
Nebuchadnezzar's dream, pinpointed the time for the
Messiah. Daniel had clearly stated that during the fourth king-
dom God would establish His Kingdom:

> "Then there will be a fourth kingdom… in the days
> of those kings the God of heaven will set up a king-
> dom which will never be destroyed…"
> (Daniel 2:40, 44)

Daniel had clearly identified these four kingdoms. It was
common Jewish knowledge that the first kingdom was
Babylon, the second was the Medo-Persian, the third Grecian,
and the fourth was the Roman. So, at some time in the fourth
kingdom, during the span of the Roman empire and its rulers,
the Jewish people began to look for their promised Messiah
with great expectation. By the time of Jesus, there had come
numerous false Christs and Jesus knew there were many to
come afterwards. Luke commented on the mood of the people as they awaited the expected Messiah:

> "The people were in a state of expectation and all
> wondering in their hearts about John, as to whether
> he might be the Christ." (Luke 3:15)

Following the death of Jesus, many false messiahs
appeared in Israel. The Lord had warned the Church not to be
caught off guard. False messiahs came on the scene early in
the Church's history. As Luke wrote the Book of Acts, he
made several references to the impostors. Simon was the best
known:

> "Now there was a certain man named Simon, who
> formerly was practicing magic in the city, and aston-

ishing the people of Samaria, claiming to be someone great; and they all, from smallest to greatest,
were giving attention to him, saying, 'This man is
what is called the Great Power of God.'" (Acts 8:9-10)

Secular historians have recorded the activities and teachings
of many false messiahs. Josephus writes:

"...a certain impostor named Theudas persuaded a
great number to follow him to the river Jordan which
he claimed would divide for their passage." [4]

Josephus continues:

"The land was overrun with magicians, seducers, and
impostors, who drew the people after them in multitudes into solitudes and deserts, to see signs and miracles which they promised to show by the power
of God." [5]

During the reign of the Roman procurator Felix from
A.D. 52-60 there were many of these impostors who preyed
upon the gullibility of the people. In order to deal with these
charlatans, Thomas Newton observes that:

"many of them were apprehended and killed every
day. They seduced great numbers of people still
expecting the Messiah..." [6]

According to Kik, the early Church father Irenaeus tells
that Simon:

---

[4] Flavius Josephus, "Antiquities of the Jews," pp. 22-429 in The Complete Works of
Josephus, tr. William Whiston, (Grand Rapids: Kregel, 1981), XX.V.1, 418.

[5] Albert Barnes, "Matthew," Notes, Explanatory and Practical, on the New Testament, eds.
Ingram Cobbin and E. Henderson, (London: James S. Virtue, n.d.), p. 251.

[6] Thomas Newton, Dissertations on the Prophecies, Which Have Remarkably Been
Fulfilled at this Time and are Fulfilling in the World, three vols., 5th ed., (London: The
Bible and Crown in St. Paul's Church-Yard, 1777), vol. 2, p. 239.

"Claimed to be the Son of God and creator of angels." [7]

Kik notes that Jerome, the fourth century translator and commentator of the scriptures quotes Simon Magus as saying:

"I am the Word of God, I am the Comforter, I am Almighty, I am all there is of God..." [7]

Christian historians and theologians have long recognized the problem the early Church faced with false messiahs. Spence and Excell relate the following:

"There were doubtless many false Messiahs whose names are little known, and critics have enumerated twenty-nine such. The pretensions of these persons were generally admitted, and their adherents were commonly few and uninfluential...But we may observe that the warning may include such deceivers as Simon Magus and those many false teachers who vexed the early church, and, without assuming the name of Christ, did Satan's work by undermining the faith." [8]

Not only was there Messianic expectation among the Jewish people, but all over the world. The Roman historian Tacitus spoke of the world wide expectation of a King rising from Israel who would be the King and the ruler of the world. And so, Jesus warned these four disciples:

"Many will come in my name claiming, 'I am the Christ." (Matthew 24:5)

---

[7] Kik, p. 92.
[8] H. D. M. Spence and Joseph F. Excell eds., "Matthew," in The Pulpit Commentary Vol. 15, (Grand Rapids: Wm. B. Eerdmans, n.d.), p. 431.

Misleading Sign #2
Wars and Rumors of Wars

*"You will hear of wars and rumors of wars, but see
to it that you are not alarmed. Such things must
happen, but the end is still to come..."*
(Matthew 24:6)

When Jesus gave this warning the Roman Empire was in
an extended time of peace. However, within a few years, the
Empire was filled with "wars and rumors of wars." Four
emperors, Nero, Galba, Otho and Vitellius suffered violent
deaths in the space of eighteen months. As a result of these
changes in government, there were disruptions throughout
the empire. Allegiances were formed around the various
emperors and Rome was fractured with bloody violence as the
consequence.

DeMar points out that Tacitus, the Roman Historian of
this period speaks of:

"...the tumult of the period with phrases such as 'disturbances in Germany', 'commotions in Africa',
'commotions in Thrace', 'insurrections in Gaul',
'intrigues among the Parthians', 'the war in Britain,'
and 'the war in Armenia.' Wars were fought from one
end of the empire to the other. With this description
we can see further fulfillment: 'For nation will rise
against nation, and kingdom against kingdom."
(Matthew 24:7) [9]

In his history of this era Josephus speaks of how com-
monplace Roman civil wars had become:

"I have omitted to give an exact account of them,
because they are well known by all, and they are
described by a great number of Greek and Roman

[9] DeMar, Last Days: Obsession, pp. 62-63.

authors; yet for the sake of the connection of mat-
ters, and that my history may not be incoherent, I
have just touched upon everything briefly." [10]

Throughout this period there were constant rumors of
wars. Josephus recorded both the Bardanes and the Vologeses
declared war on the Jews, but it was never carried out. [11] He
also says Vitellius, governor of Syria, declared war against
Aretas, king of Arabia, and wished to lead his army through
Palestine. But the war never materialized. [12]

"...wars and rumors of wars..." (Matthew 24:6)

Also, throughout the region of Israel there was tremendous resistance to the Roman occupation. According to theologian Alexander Keith the great "Roman Peace" was
very fragile:

"The Jews resisted the erection of the statue of
Caligula in the Temple; and such was the dread of
Roman resentment, that the fields remained unculti-
vated. At Caesarea, the Jews and Syrians contended
for the mastery of the city. Twenty thousand of the
former were put to death, and the rest were expelled.
Every city in Syria was then divided into armies, and
multitudes were slaughtered. Alexandria and
Damascus presented a similar scene of bloodshed.
About fifty thousand Jews fell in the former, and ten
thousand in the latter. The Jewish nation rebelled
against the Romans..." [13]

---

10 Flavius Josephus, "The Wars of the Jews," in The Complete Works of Josephus, pp. 429-
605, tr. William Whiston, (Grand Rapids: Kregel, 1981), IV.IX.2, 540.

11 Josephus, "Antiquities," XX.III. p. 417.

12 Josephus, "Antiquities," XVIII. p. 382.

13 Alexander Keith, The Evidence of the Truth of the Christian Religion Derived from the
Literal Fulfillment of Prophecy; Particularly as Illustrated by the History of the Jews, And
by the Discoveries of Recent Travelers, (Philadelphia: Presbyterian Board of Publication,
n.d.), p. 59-60.

In the Olivet Discourse, Jesus was preparing His champions. These men would be the foundation stones upon which Christianity would be built. They had to understand the occurrences which would radically shake their world over the next forty years. They must not be misled, for they had to lead the New Covenant people of God through this period of upheaval and transition.

Misleading Sign #3
International Turmoil and Conflict

"Nation will rise against nation, and kingdom
against kingdom." (Matthew 24:7)

They were not to be frightened. Nation rising against nation would not be the end, but only part of the beginning of birth pains. Jesus was preparing His disciples for events which would and *did take place during their lives!* They would lead the infant Church through a generation which would be constantly exploding. Every day would be filled with dangers. If they were not clear concerning the ultimate will of heaven in these situations they would easily be disheartened and lose faith.

Tacitus, the Roman historian of the period describes the generation between the resurrection of Jesus and the destruction of Jerusalem in A.D. 70:

> "I enter upon a work fertile in vicissitudes, stained with the blood of battles, embroiled with dissensions, horrible even in the interval of peace. Four princes slain; three civil wars, more with foreign enemies, and sometimes both at once; prosperity in the East, disasters in the West; Illyricum disturbed; the Gauls ready to revolt; Britain conquered, and again lost; Samaritans and Suevians conspiring against us; the

Dacians renowned for defeats given and sustained; the Parathions almost aroused to arms by a counterfeit Nero. Italy afflicted with calamities unheard of, or recurring only after a long interval; cities overwhelmed or swallowed up in the fertile region of Campania; Rome itself laid waste by fire, the most ancient Temples destroyed, the very capitol burned by its citizens..." [14]

When Jesus gave the Olivet Discourse the world was at peace. Rome ruled. Over the next forty years, the whole world exploded into constant conflict—just as the Lord had warned His disciples it would.

Commenting on the fact that this verse of scriptures was fulfilled in the lifetime of these four disciples, DeMar writes:

"But what about world conditions? Aren't we seeing prophecy being fulfilled right before our eyes? This protest is offered when people are hit with an interpretation that no longer fits their doctrinal views. They shift from the clear teaching of Scripture to current events. The Bible is then read through the lens of today's newsprint, a form of 'newspaper exegesis.'

Our nation, and every nation, could go through the most tumultuous upheaval that history has ever experienced, and this still would not mean that Jesus was returning soon. For date setters, history is ignored; the result is that the Church experiences wild gyrations in the field of biblical prophecy." [15]

[14] Tacitus, The Histories, 4 vols, trans, Clifford H. Moore, (Cambridge, MA: Harvard University, 1962), 16.13, pp. 5-7.
[15] DeMar, Last Days: Obsession, pp. 3-4.

Misleading Sign # 4
Famines and Pestilence

"...and in various places there will be famines."
(Matthew 24:7)

Luke writes in Acts 11:28 of the famine which occurred throughout the Roman empire during the reign of Claudius, A.D. 41-54. Josephus, Suetonius, and Tacitus all agree. In fact, four different famines are recorded during the reign of Claudius in Rome, Palestine and Greece. Josephus insists the famine was so severe that many died in Jerusalem.[16] Each of the historians wrote of a single autumn in which thirty thousand died of famine and pestilence in Rome.[17] Raging epidemic diseases like the plague killed thousands in Babylon in A.D. 40,[18] and in Italy in A.D. 66.[19]

The New Testament further records the Apostle Paul's efforts to gather special offerings from the Churches throughout the Roman Empire to help relieve the suffering of the believers in Judea due to famine.

These had to be trying times for the Church. For forty years their entire world was disintegrating before their eyes with little to hold on to except the prophecy Jesus had given on the Temple mount and the promises He had given them on various occasions that all of these things would happen in their day and that some of them would live to see His Kingdom manifested in power and glory. Yet, these promises sustained them and led them to victory!

---

[16] Josephus, "Antiquities," XX.II.5, p. 416.
[17] Spence and Excell, p. 432.
[18] Josephus, "Antiquities," XVIII.IX.8, p. 395.
[19] Tacitus, 16.13.

Misleading Sign #5
Earthquakes

"...and in various places there will be... earthquakes." (Matthew 24:7)

Jesus was not speaking of world-wide earthquakes at the end of history, but rather in "various places" in their own day. The number of earthquakes during the lives of the disciples was astounding. According to Kik:

"There were earthquakes in Crete, Smyrna, Miletus, Chios, Samos, Laodicea, Hierapolis, Colosse, Campania, Rome, and Judea. It is interesting to note that the city of Pompeii was much damaged by an earthquake occurring on February 5, 63 A.D." [21]

Keith also comments on this phenomenon:

"Josephus describes an earthquake in Judea of such magnitude 'that the constitution of the universe was confounded for the destruction of men.' He goes on to write that this earthquake was 'no common' calamity, indicating that God Himself had brought it about for a special purpose." [22]

Once again, it was Josephus and Tacitus who wrote of earthquakes in Rome, Crete, Laodicea and at Jerusalem. All of these occurred during the lives of the four disciples.

In his commentary on this passage, theologian Edward Hayes Plumptre writes:

"Perhaps no period in the world's history has ever been so marked by these convulsions as that which

---

[21] Kik, p. 93.
[22] Keith, p. 60.

intervenes between the Crucifixion and the destruction of Jerusalem." [23]

Since our Lord was speaking of the generation between A.D. 30 and A.D. 70, there is no reason to project any prophetic importance to earthquakes in our modern day. However, the prophecy speculators are undaunted by the truth that this prophecy of Jesus has already been fulfilled.

Misleading Sign #6
Disturbances in the Heavens

"...and there will be terrors and great signs from heaven." (Luke 21:11)

Matthew's version of the Olivet Discourse does not mention this warning. It is found only in Luke's version. But it is found in the same setting as Matthew's with the same prophecy concerning the destruction of the Temple.

It is in this context that Luke gives us the added words of warning: "terrors and great signs from heaven," followed by the identical warning concerning persecutions as recorded in Matthew and Mark.

Comets appearing in the heavens were often taken by ancient cultures as warnings of some approaching calamity. They were often considered bad omens of some pending change in existing political and social structures.

Jesus was warning these men about "terrors" and "signs in the heavens" that would appear in their lifetime that could possibly terrify and mislead them. DeMar asks the pertinent question:

---

[23] Edward Hayes Plumptre, "The Gospel According to St. Matthew," Ellicott's Commentary on the Whole Bible, ed. Charles John Ellicott, 8 vols. (Grand Rapids: Zondervan, 1959), 6: 146.

"Were there any 'signs from heaven' prior to A.D. 70 that would be a fulfillment of Luke 21:11?" [24]

DeMar points out that during the reign of Nero, a comet appeared around A.D. 60 which caused the Romans to speculate that a change in the political scene was about to take place. DeMar quotes from Nigel Calder's book, *The Comet Is Coming!: The Feverish Legacy of Mr. Halley*:

"The historian Tacitus wrote: 'As if Nero were already dethroned, men began to ask who might be his successor.' [25]

Calder once more:

"Nero took no chances as another historian, Suetonius, related: 'All children of the condemned man, were banished from Rome, and then starved to death or poisoned.' The policy worked like a charm. Nero survived that comet by several years." [26]

DeMar once again:

"Nero may have thought that he was finished with warnings from heaven. History records Halley's Comet appeared in A.D. 66. Soon after Nero committed suicide!" [27]

Halley's Comet has been linked by historians not only with Nero's death but with the destruction of Jerusalem in A.D. 70. In *Asimov's Guide to Halley's Comet* there is a reproduction of a seventeenth-century print which depicts the comet as it passes over Jerusalem. The caption reads:

---

[24] DeMar, Last Days: Obsession, p. 66.
[25] Nigel Calder, The Comet Is Coming!: The Feverish Legacy of Mr. Halley, p. 12, cited in DeMar, Last Days: Obsession, p. 66.
[26] Calder, p. 13, cited in DeMar, Last Days: Obsession, p. 66.
[27] DeMar, Last Days: Obsession, p. 66.

"Halley's Comet of A.D. 66 shown over Jerusalem...
The comet was regarded as an omen predicting the
fall of the city to the Romans which actually
occurred four years later." [28]

Not only was there Halley's Comet but it is well known
historically that Josephus recorded a number of strange phenomena in the heavens. He considered these as signs of God's
displeasure with the city and nation and omens of impending
judgment. These phenomena are described in his own words:

"Thus there was a star resembling a sword, which
stood over the city, and a comet, that continued a
whole year." [29]

He goes on to recount:

"...a certain prodigious and incredible phenomenon
appeared; I suppose the account of it would seem to
be a fable, were it not related by those that saw it,
and were not the events that followed it of so consid-
erable a nature as to deserve such signals; for, before
sun-setting, chariots and troops of soldiers in their
armor were seen running about among the clouds,
and surrounding of cities. Moreover at that feast
which we call Pentecost, as the priests were going by
night into the inner [court of the] Temple, as their
custom was, to perform their sacred ministrations,
they said that, in the first place, they felt a quaking,
and heard a great noise, and after that they heard a
sound as of a multitude, saying, "Let us remove
hence." [30]

---

[28] Isaac Asimov, <u>Asimov's Guide to Halley's Comet: The Awesome Story of Comets</u>, (New York: Walker and Co., 1985), p. 6.

[29] Josephus, "Wars," VI.V.3, p. 582.

[30] Josephus, "Wars," VI.V.3, p. 582.

These events were also reported by Tacitus:

> "In the sky appeared a vision of armies in conflict, of
> glittering armour. A sudden lightning flash from the
> clouds lit up the Temple. The doors of the holy place
> abruptly opened, a superhuman voice was heard to
> declare that the gods were leaving it, and in the same
> instant came the rushing tumult of their departure." [31]

Jesus was speaking to His disciples telling them not to be
afraid or misled by the things that would be happening in
their skies and in their day.

Misleading Sign #7
Persecution

*"Then they will deliver you to tribulation, and will
kill you, and you will be hated by all nations on
account of My name." (Matthew 24:9)*

Persecution was a way of life in the first Church. It was the
crucible in which the Church prospered. The book of Acts is
full of accounts of persecution. Peter and John were arrested
early on in their ministry, brought before the rulers of the
Jewish nation and warned not to speak in the name of Jesus.
Later they were arrested, thrown in prison, beaten and commanded not to preach in the name of the Lord. Eventually
Stephen was martyred and "great persecution" broke out
against the young Church under the direction of Saul of
Tarsus. To please the Jews, Herod had James, who had been
with Jesus on the Mount of Olives and heard these very words
of warning, put to death with the sword. Herod attempted to

---

31 Tacitus, The Histories, translated by Kenneth Wellesley, (New York: Penguin Books,
1964, 1975, p. 279.), cited in David Chilton, Paradise Restored: A Biblical Theology of
Dominion, (Tyler, TX: Reconstruction, 1985), p.290 note #35.

do the same with Peter, but God intervened in response to the Church's prayers and delivered him.

The Apostle Paul testified about his sufferings for the name:

> "Five times I received from the Jews thirty-nine lashes. Three times I was beaten with rods, once I was stoned... I have been on frequent journeys, in dangers from rivers, dangers from robbers, dangers from my countrymen, dangers from the Gentiles."
> (2 Corinthians 11:24-26)

In A.D. 66, John, the apostle of the Lamb, wrote of his companionship with these first-century disciples in the persecution of the period:

> "I, John, your brother and fellow partaker in the tribulation and kingdom and perseverance which are in Jesus, was on the island called Patmos, because of the word of God and the testimony of Jesus."
> (Revelation 1:9)

In the second century, Tertullian wrote of the persecution of these first Christians:

> "There was war against the very name." [32]

Just as Jesus had warned, these very disciples were delivered up to tribulation, some were killed, and all were hated for the sake of His name.

DeMar quotes from Thomas Newton concerning the fulfillment of Jesus' prediction to these men on the Mount of Olives:

[32] Keith, p. 61.

"Some are 'brought before rulers and kings,' as Paul before Gallio, (xviii.12) Felix, (xxiv) Festus and Agrippa, (xxv)...Some are beaten, as Paul and Silas: (xvi.23)...But if we would look farther, we have a more melancholy proof of the truth of this prediction, in the persecutions under Nero, in which (besides numberless other Christians) fell those two champions of our faith, St. Peter and St. Paul." [33]

Tacitus records that Nero blamed the Christians for the burning of Rome and persecuted them for it:

"Tacitus says that Nero, for the conflagration of Rome, persecuted the Christians, "a race detested for their crimes..." [34]

Gibbon writes in his great history of Roman decline:

"A candid but rational inquiry into the progress and establishment of Christianity may be considered as a very essential part of the history of the Roman empire...a pure and humble religion gently insinuated itself into the minds of men, grew up in silence and obscurity, derived new vigor from opposition, and finally erected the triumphant banner of the Cross on the ruins of the Capitol." [35]

God would use persecution of the first generation Church to get them out of Jerusalem, and into all the world.

Certainly this does not mean that there has not been tribulation and persecution at other periods of Church history, or that there may not be in the future. There have been great heroes of the faith who have suffered for the sake of His

---

[33] Thomas Newton, vol. 2, pp. 252-253.

[34] Henry Alford, The New Testament for English Readers, (London: Deighton, Bell and Co., 1868), p. 163.

[35] Edward Gibbon, The Decline and Fall of Rome, abridgment by D. M. Low, (New York: Harcourt, Brace and Company, 1960), p. 143.

name in every age and there will be heroes of the faith in the future. What it does mean is that between A.D. 30 and A.D. 70, the tribulation which these men and their fellow believers actually suffered was the fulfillment of the prophecy of Jesus in this passage of scripture.

Misleading Sign #8
The Falling Away of Believers

"At that time, many will fall away from the faith and will deliver up one another and hate one another." (Matthew 24:10)

Because of incredible persecution, the first generation Church was constantly struggling to retain its converts. Many fell away. The Apostle Paul was repeatedly faced with betrayal from his followers during that first generation:

> "You are aware of the fact that all who are in Asia turned away from me..." (1 Timothy 1:15)

> "...Demas, having loved this present world, has deserted me and gone to Thessalonica; Crescens has gone to Galatia, Titus to Dalmatia...Alexander, the coppersmith did me much harm."
> (1 Timothy 4:10, 14)

Christians turned on Christians! Even Tacitus openly wrote of this betrayal, and how it was used by the enemies of the Church to destroy so many believers:

> "First those were seized who confessed that they were Christians; and then on their information a vast multitude was convicted and barbarously executed." [36]

---

[36] Newton, vol. 2, p. 254, see also Tacitus <u>Annals</u> xv 44.

As the disciples sat there that day, looking down on the Temple and the city from the Mount of Olives, Jesus was warning them. Before their city and the Temple which was then standing would be destroyed there would come a falling away among His followers. Jesus was not speaking to some future generation who would be alive in "the last days" of the Church age. He was warning the disciples and their generation who was at that moment living through the last days of Israel as the covenant nation.

The apostasy which Jesus said would come, came just as He had predicted and before the end of that first century. And while it is true that throughout the history of the Church there have been other periods of decline and apostasy, the Lord's Church will not fail in her purpose. Because of her Founder and through the "all-authority" of her glorious Head, the Church will ultimately succeed in her mission of discipling the nations and filling the earth with the glory of God.

Misleading Sign #9
False Prophets

"Many false prophets will arise, and will mislead many." (Matthew 24:11)

Josephus records that the Jews were deceived continually by fanatics who professed to be the Messiah. They promised Israel deliverance from Rome and immediate victory. Many believed.[37] Reporting on the abundance of false prophets who deceived and deluded the Jewish people he writes:

> "There was also another body of wicked men gotten together, not so impure in their actions, but more wicked in their intentions, who laid waste the happy state of the city no less than did these murderers. These were such men as deceived and deluded the

---

[37] Josephus, "Wars," VI.V.2-3, p. 582.

people under pretense of divine inspiration, but were for procuring innovations and changes of the government, and these prevailed with the multitude to act like madmen, and went before them into the wilderness, as pretending that God would there show them the signals of liberty..." [38]

Later in the same writings Josephus tells of a particular false prophet:

"...There was an Egyptian false prophet that did the Jews more mischief than the former; for he was a cheat, and pretended to be a prophet also, and got together thirty thousand men that were deluded by him; these he led round about from the wilderness to the mount which was called the Mount of Olives, and was ready to break into Jerusalem by force from that place; and if he could but once conquer the Roman garrison and the people, he intended to domineer over them by the assistance of those guards of his that were to break into the city with him..." [39]

As an eyewitness to the siege of Jerusalem culminating in A.D. 70, Josephus wrote:

"The tyrannical zealots who ruled the city suborned many false prophets to declare that aid would be given to the people from heaven. This was done to prevent them from attempting to desert, and to inspire confidence in God." [40]

Not only the apostate Jewish nation, but the early Church also had its plague of false prophets. Judeaizers and Gnostics desperately tried to destroy the work of the apostles. They deceived many within the Church. The Apostle Peter, who

[38] Josephus, "Wars," II.XII.4, p. 483.
[39] Josephus, "Wars," II.XII.5, p. 483
[40] Josephus, "Wars," VI.V.2., p. 582.

was with Jesus on the Mount of Olives and heard the Lord's warning of false prophets wrote:

> "But false prophets rose among the people, just as there will also be false teachers among you, who will secretly introduce destructive heresies, even denying the Master who bought them, bringing swift destruction upon themselves. And many will follow their sensuality, and because of them the way of the truth will be maligned; and in their greed they will exploit you with false words..." (2 Peter 2:1-3)

Peter was not speaking of some future day. He was writing of what would happen to that first generation of believers. As Jesus had warned earlier, Peter announced false prophets would rise up among them and "malign the truth" and "in their greed" would "exploit" that generation of Christians.

The Apostle Paul described the Judeaizing teachers of his day as:

> "False apostles, deceitful workers, disguising themselves as apostles of Christ." (2 Corinthians 11:13)

The Ephesian elders were warned against "savage wolves" who would come in among them and who would not spare the flock. Paul told them that from their own number and in their own lifetime men would arise "speaking perverse things, to draw away disciples after themselves." (Acts 20:29-30)

Paul warned Timothy against the false prophets Hymenaeus and Philetus who were falsely teaching that the resurrection of the body had already taken place. (2 Timothy 2:16-18)

The Apostle John, who was also on the Mount of Olives with the Lord, wrote of his own generation:

"Many false prophets have gone out into the
world..." (1 John 4:1)

John did not say that many false prophets would go out
into the world some day. He told his generation of believers
they had already gone into the world, just as Jesus had warned
they would.

One of these false prophets against whom John was warning the Church of his day was Cerinthus. Cerinthus was the
leader of a first-century Judaistic cult who came to be regarded by the early Church Fathers as "the Arch-heretic." He was
identified by these Church Fathers as one of the "false apostles" who opposed the Apostle Paul. It was against Cerinthus
and others like him that Paul wrote:

"But even though we, or an angel from heaven,
should preach to you a gospel contrary to that which
we have preached to you, let him be accursed."
(Galatians 1:8 NASV)

Paul goes on in his letter to the Galatians to refute the
legalistic heresies of Cerinthus and his followers.

According to Chilton:

"...Cerinthus was a Jew who joined the Church and
began drawing Christians away from the orthodox
faith. He taught that a lessor deity and not the true
God, had created the world... this meant also a
denial of the Incarnation, since God would never
take upon Himself a physical body and a real human
personality... Cerinthus... declared that Jesus had
merely been an ordinary man, not born of a virgin;
that "the Christ" (a heavenly spirit) had descended
upon the man Jesus at His baptism (enabling Him to
perform miracles), but then left Him again at the cru-

cifixion. Cerinthus also advocated a doctrine of justi-
fication by works – in particular, the absolute necessity of observing the ceremonial ordinances of the
Old Covenant in order to be saved." [41]

In addition to these Judeaizing tendencies and contrary to
the teaching of the original Apostles, Cerinthus appears to be
the first person in history to teach that the Second Coming
would usher in a literal reign of Christ in Jerusalem for a thousand years. He claimed that an angel had revealed this doctrine to him.

The Apostle Paul sternly opposed the Cerinthian heresy in
his writings. And according to the early Church Fathers the
Apostle John wrote his Gospel as well as his letters with
Cerinthus especially in mind. We are told that on one occasion as John entered a public bathhouse he saw this false
prophet and false apostle ahead of him. Immediately the
Apostle John turned around and ran from the bathhouse
declaring: "Let us flee, lest the building fall down; for
Cerinthus, the enemy of the truth, is inside!"

Misleading Sign #10
"Lawlessness is Increased…" Matthew 24:12

The New Testament is filled with examples of the fulfillment of this very warning before that first generation of
believers had passed away. The Church at Jerusalem faced
tremendous illegal persecution. Throughout the Roman
Empire lawlessness was increasingly rampant. The history of
this period of the Roman Empire and especially of its emperors reveals clearly that there was a rising flood of lawlessness.
As DeMar points out: "The names of Caligula and Nero are
synonymous with 'lawlessness'." [42] Consequently, not only in
Jerusalem but everywhere throughout the whole of the empire
Christians were illegally accused, illegally tried and illegally

---

[41] Chilton, Paradise Restored, p. 111.
[42] DeMar, Last Days: Obsession, p. 70.

executed. Neither the law of Rome nor of Israel protected them. The Apostle Paul often cites throughout his letters his many imprisonments, beatings, scourgings and stonings.

The increase of lawlessness was not only rampant outside the Church but was also a growing problem within the believing community. Paul was shocked at the behavior of the Corinthian Church.

> "It is actually reported that there is immorality among you, and immorality of such a kind as does not exist even among the Gentiles, that someone has his father's wife. And you have become arrogant, and have not mourned instead, in order that the one who had done this deed might be removed from your midst." (1 Corinthians 5:1-2 NASV)

Many other scriptural examples could be given.

Misleading Sign #11
Love Growing Cold

> *"…most people's love will grow cold."*
> *(Matthew 24:12)*

The New American Standard Version makes a clear connection between the increase of lawlessness throughout the world of that day and the loss or the failure of the love on the part of many. Because of the persecution the Church experienced times of betrayal, abandonment and a lack of commitment to each other. Jesus had warned these four on the Mount of Olives:

> "They will deliver you to tribulation, and will kill you, and you will be hated of all nations on account of My name. And at that time many will fall away and will deliver up one another and hate one another." (Matthew 24:9-10)

"Brother will deliver up brother to death, and a father his child; and children will rise up against parents and have them put to death." (Mark 13:12)

"You will be delivered up even by parents and brothers and relatives and friends, and they will put some of you to death..." (Luke 21:16)

Concerning the cause and effect relationship between the increase in iniquity or lawlessness and the chilling of love, DeMar quotes from Newton:

"By reason of these trials and persecutions from without, and these apostasies and false prophets from within, the love of many to Christ and his doctrine, and also their love to one another shall wax cold. Some shall openly desert the faith, (as ver. 10;) others shall corrupt it, (as ver. 11;) and others again, (as here) shall grow indifferent to it. And (not to mention other instances) who can hear St. Paul complaining at Rome, (2 Timothy iv. 16,) that 'at his first answer no man stood with him, but all men forsook him'; who can hear the divine author of the Epistle to the Hebrews, exhorting them, (x. 25,) "not to forsake the assembling of themselves together, as the manner of some is"; and not conclude the event to have sufficiently justified our Saviour's prediction?" [43]

DeMar continues:

"Through it all the Church was not defeated. The Church continues to this day while all of its first-century enemies lie in the dust. In our day new enemies are equally intent on destroying the Church. Their end is equally sure. Seeing how God fulfilled this extraordinary prophecy should bolster our faith that

[43] Newton, vol. 2, p. 255.

He will do the same for His church as it nears the twenty-first century. If non-Christian "folly [was made] obvious to all" in the first century (2 Timothy 3:9), can we expect any less in our century?" [44]

Throughout His enumeration of false signs, Jesus continually comforted His disciples:

"See to it that no one mislead you… see that you are not frightened, for these things must take place, but that is not yet the end… all these things are merely the beginnings of birth pangs." (Matthew 24:4-8)

He ended this section of the Olivet Discourse with these ominous words:

"But the one who endures to the end, it is he who shall be saved." (Matthew 24:13)

Time was running out for the apostate nation and its spiritually bankrupt leaders and their religious system. These disciples would live through the transition. Some of them would live to see the ending of the Old Covenant nation and the beginning of the New Covenant people. It would be a period of tremendous upheaval, incredible change and continual tribulation. Yet, these disciples would establish the Church of Jesus Christ which not only survived, but conquered. The Lord had prepared them not to be deterred by spurious signs. They obeyed!

---

[44] DeMar, Last Days: Obsession, p. 70.

4

THE STIPULATION FOR THE SIGN

The disciples hung on every word. Jesus was detailing for them the most important series of events in history—and they were to be major participants in those spectacular moments. Having vividly described the spurious signs of the Kingdom and before answering the disciples' strategic questions, the Lord paused to place one demand upon His followers. Specifically, to His twelve disciples gathered on the Mount of Olives, He declared a single stipulation which they must fulfill before the sign of the Kingdom would take place:

> "And this Gospel of the Kingdom shall be preached
> in the whole world for a witness to all nations, and
> then the end shall come." (Matthew 24:14)

These particular disciples were to preach "this Gospel of the Kingdom" to the entire Jewish world scattered throughout the nations of the Roman Empire and then the end of the age would come—the end of the Old Covenant age—the end of the age of Moses.

The Gospel of the Kingdom was the Gospel of Jesus Christ. It was not the Gospel of an earthly, political, Jewish Kingdom. It was a Gospel of a heavenly Kingdom. It was the Gospel of Salvation both to the Jews and the Gentiles.

Seated on the Mount of Olives that day, anticipating His death, burial, resurrection and ascension to the Father, Jesus readied these disciples to take the Gospel of the Kingdom to the entire Jewish world before the destruction of Jerusalem. Based upon the response of these four disciples to the stipulation of the Lord Jesus, it is clear that they believed the Gospel of the Kingdom was the only Gospel. They believed the Gospel of the Kingdom was the Gospel of Grace—the Gospel of Salvation.

Throughout His ministry the Lord Jesus had unfolded the details of the Gospel of the Kingdom. It was not new or novel. Indeed, it was based upon the great prophetic Messianic promises of the Old Testament. One of those promises was made to King David:

"The Lord has sworn to David,
A truth from which He will not turn back;

Of the fruit of your body, I will set upon your throne." (Psalm 132:11)

This fruit of David's body would not only be the son of David, He would also be the Son of God:

"I will be a Father to Him and He will be a Son to Me..." (2 Samuel 7:14)

David prophetically saw God install David's descendant—a man, the anointed, the Christ, the Son of God—upon David's throne. This was the common expectation of the Jewish people in the first century. It was the Apostle Peter who authoritatively interpreted David's prophetic vision.

Preaching his apostolic message at Pentecost, Peter declared that David:

> "...was a prophet, and knew that God had sworn to
> him with an oath to seat one of his descendants
> upon his throne, he looked ahead and spoke of the
> resurrection of the Christ..." (Acts 2:30-31)

According to Peter, David did not speak of Christ sitting upon David's throne at the second coming, as many insist, but he "spoke of the resurrection of the Christ". Peter makes no mention of the second coming in his Pentecost proclamation. The Kingdom of Christ would begin with His resurrection and ascension.

Jesus would sit on David's throne—but not on earth, and not in earthly Jerusalem! Contrary to the Jewish messianic expectation, and because of His resurrection and ascension, the Lord would reign from the throne of David in heaven. That was the message of the resurrection. It was the heart of the Gospel of the Kingdom. And the Gospel of the Kingdom was the heart of the early Church—they had no other message!

Prior to the death, burial and resurrection of the Lord the message was "the kingdom of heaven is at hand." It was at hand because Jesus was at hand. After His death, the Kingdom was not postponed, it was established in His resurrection, ascension and enthronement at God's right hand in heaven! Peter continued:

> "This Jesus God raised up again...therefore having
> been exalted to the right hand of God, and having
> received from the Father the promise of the Holy
> Spirit, He has poured forth this which you both see
> and hear. For it was not David who ascended into
> heaven, but He himself says: 'the Lord said to my
> Lord, sit at My right hand until I make thine enemies
> a footstool for Thy feet...'" (Acts 2:32-36)

At Pentecost Peter boldly proclaimed the good news of the Kingdom. Jesus had been raised up and exalted to the place of authority and power at the right hand of God. He had received the Holy Spirit who was being poured out in His name to raise up and create a New Israel. That new Israel would be empowered by the Holy Spirit to disciple the nations just as the prophets had promised. The outpouring of the Holy Spirit on the day of Pentecost was the Holy anointing oil poured out upon the head of God's resurrected, ascended, glorified, enthroned king in heaven which also flowed down upon His waiting body of believers in the upper room in Jerusalem, as a supernatural demonstration to the whole House of Israel:

"That God has made Him both Lord and Christ—this Jesus whom you crucified." (Acts 2:36)

Therefore the message of the early Church became the good news that Jesus of Nazareth is God's Christ, His anointed King! He had been declared by His resurrection to be Lord and Christ. He had ascended to the place of all authority and all power at God's right hand. He is presently exercising all the rights and privileges of deity and is therefore ruling and judging the nations today as King of Kings and Lord of Lords.

The Gospel of the Kingdom according to these first Apostles was the good news that "Jesus is the Christ" which meant to them "He is the King." They proclaimed that His name is above every name. In His name is salvation. In His name is forgiveness of sin. In His name is healing and deliverance from every oppression of evil—spirit, soul and body. In His name the Spirit is being poured out upon all flesh in order that He might fill all things and bring forth the New Creation. In His name the full blessings of Abraham and the sure mercies of David are coming upon all who call upon Him in faith. And in His name the nations are presently being brought under His righteous rule and governmental discipline. This is the significance of the resurrection as the risen Christ appeared to the eleven on a mountain in Galilee and declared:

> "All authority has been given to Me in heaven and on earth. Go therefore and make disciples of all the nations, baptizing them in the name of the Father and the Son and the Holy Spirit, teaching them to observe all that I commanded you; and lo, I am with you always, even to the end of the age."
> (Matthew 28:18-20)

His "all authority" was not only in heaven, but also on earth. Therefore His Kingship or government over all the nations had not been postponed to some future, earthly, millennial Kingdom yet to be established. Rather, it has already been securely established by His resurrection! This was the Lord's own declaration to these original apostolic leaders.

Obviously, they believed Him. Their constant theme was the resurrected, ascended King Jesus:

> "With great power the apostles were giving witness to the resurrection of the Lord Jesus..." (Acts 4:33)

The resurrection was not just philosophy to the disciples. They saw it as the validation of all they believed—proof of the fulfillment of all the Old Testament promises of the Messianic Kingdom and the installation of Jesus as King on the throne of His father David—in heaven! David had seen that same installation:

> "I have installed My King
> Upon Zion, My holy mountain."

"I will surely tell of *the decree* of the Lord:
He said to Me, 'Thou art My Son
Today I have begotten Thee...'"

"Now therefore, O kings, show discernment...
Worship the Lord...
Do homage to the Son, lest He become angry, and
you perish..." (Psalm 2:6-11)

The disciples fully believed the prophetic vision of David concerning God's Christ. They saw David's prophetic vision as the foundation of the Gospel of the Kingdom. In the resurrection of Jesus of Nazareth the Father had raised His anointed Son and in His ascension He had seated Him upon the throne of David in heaven as King! This was the message of these early Apostles.

The Apostle Paul joined with the disciples and insisted:

"We preach to you the good news of the promise
made to the fathers, that God has fulfilled this
promise to our children in that He raised up Jesus, as
it is also written in the second Psalm, 'Thou art My
Son; today I have begotten Thee'." (Acts 13:32-33)

The rationale behind the Gospel of the Kingdom which these first disciples preached was David's second Psalm—the Son of God was reigning as King of Kings and Lord of Lords. The message was a clear commandment. Upon the basis of Jesus being the resurrected Christ, the nations of the earth must either repent of their lawlessness and rebellion and receive Him, coming under His rule, enjoying the blessings of His Kingdom, or come under His judgments and perish!

These first Apostles recognized fully that the Gospel was the "good news" of God Himself—His very own covenantal decree. Therefore for them salvation was not an option; it was a commandment:

"Now therefore, O kings, show discernment; Take warning, O judges of the earth. Worship the Lord with reverence, and rejoice with trembling. Do homage to the Son, lest He become angry, and you perish in the way, For His wrath may soon be kindled. How blessed are all who seek refuge in Him!" (Psalm 2:10-12)

Through David, the Lord God Almighty prophetically warned the kings and rulers of the nations of the earth to obey His resurrection decree and submit themselves fully to His anointed King, "lest He become angry" and His judgment fall upon them "in the way."

Peter and the other Apostles understood the Gospel. They recognized it as a commandment which all civil governments and all ethnic groups must obey. Based upon the demands of the Gospel of the Kingdom, Peter boldly proclaimed to the rulers and elders of Israel shortly after Pentecost:

"If we are on trial today for a benefit done to a sick man, as to how this man has been made well, let it be known to all of you and to all the people of Israel, that by the name of Jesus Christ the Nazarene, whom you crucified, whom God raised from the dead—by this name this man stands here before you in good health.

He is the stone which was rejected by you, the builders, but which became the very corner stone. And there is salvation in no one else; for there is no other name under heaven that has been given among men, by which we must be saved."(Acts 4:9-12)

This was a powerful proclamation of the Gospel of the Kingdom by this simple fisherman Apostle. After having used the keys of the Kingdom to heal a man born lame, in awesome demonstration of the power and authority of the name of Christ, Peter courageously proclaimed God's sovereign decree. God had raised this Jesus of Nazareth from the dead, thereby exalting Him and giving Him a name above every name in heaven and earth. This Jesus is God's King!

Jesus clearly instructed His disciples that before the judgment of God could come upon apostate Israel and bring about the end of the Old Covenant nation, this particular Gospel of the Kingdom must be preached in all the world of the disciples' day. Through the preaching of this Gospel, the Lord would first gather from among the nations of the Roman Empire a believing remnant of Jews who, together with the believing Gentiles, would comprise the New Covenant people of God—the Church of Jesus Christ. Then, after the remnant of believing Jews had been gathered, His judgment would be poured out:

"...then the end will come." (Matthew 24:14)

On the basis of Israel's rejection of the Gospel, the Kingdom of God would be taken from the apostate Jewish nation and given to "a nation" which would bring forth its fruit. The Old Covenant nation would end! This was the end about which Moses, Isaiah, Ezekiel, Daniel, Hosea, Joel, Amos, Zachariah and Malachi had prophesied. The end of Old Covenant Israel would be the sign to the rest of the world, to the Gentile nations, that Jesus of Nazareth was indeed the Christ—God's anointed King!

Jesus had taught this principle earlier that very day. Speaking to the Chief Priests and Pharisees He declared:

"Therefore I tell you that the kingdom of God will be taken away from you and given to a nation who will produce its fruit. He who falls on this stone will be broken to pieces, but he on whom it falls will be crushed. When the Chief Priests and Pharisees heard Jesus' parables they knew he was talking about them. They looked for a way to arrest him but they were afraid of the crowd." (Matthew 21:43-46)

The Kingdom would be taken away from the apostate nation and given to a new nation—a nation producing the fruit of the Kingdom—the Church of Jesus the King.

Some contend Jesus was speaking of the evangelistic mission of the Church which would be fulfilled just prior to His second coming. Nothing could be further from the truth. He was not speaking of the final judgment, or the end of the world. *The end* which Jesus said, "shall come," was the end of the age of Moses...the end of the Old Covenant...the end of the apostate nation of Israel. But, there was a stipulation! The end of the Old Covenant age and the beginning of the new administration of the Messiah would be brought about by the preaching of the Gospel of the Kingdom to the scattered Jews.

The Lord followed His direct warning to the Chief Priests and Pharisees with the parable of the wedding feast. In this parable, Jesus laid out the requirement for the Gospel of the Kingdom being offered to the Jewish nation before judgment would fall upon the city:

"The kingdom of heaven is like a king, who prepared a wedding banquet for his son. He sent his servants to *those who had been invited* to tell them to come. But, they refused to come." (Matthew 22:2-3)

Those who were invited to the banquet were the Jewish people, the disciples' generation of Jews. Jesus was the son. God the Father was the king. The Lord's disciples were the servants who would issue the invitations...they would preach the Gospel of the Kingdom. The servants of the King must first go to those who were the invited guests.

"He sent his servants to *those who had been invited* to the banquet to tell them to come, but they refused to come. Then he sent some more servants and said tell those who have been invited, I have prepared my dinner , my oxen and fatted calf have been butchered. Everything is ready, come to the wedding banquet." (Matthew 22:4-5)

The nation of Israel was to be offered the first invitations to the Lord's banquet. Salvation was to the Jews first. This understanding had been the hallmark of the Lord's earthly ministry. While He indicated He had "other sheep," His mission was first to the Jews to fulfill the promises God had made to their fathers, and fulfill the hope of Israel...the regathering of Israel into the believing nation. He had explicitly instructed His disciples as He sent them out to help Him in His earthly ministry:

"...Do not go in the way of the Gentiles, and do not enter any city of the Samaritans; but rather go to the lost sheep of Israel. And as you go, preach, saying, 'the Kingdom of Heaven is at hand!'"
(Matthew 10:5-6)

The mission to the Jews dominated the disciples' entire life. Jesus told them:

"...You shall not finish going through the cities of Israel, until the Son of Man comes." (Matthew 10:23)

It is obvious from their reaction that the disciples understood Jesus' stipulation. As they committed their lives to fulfilling it, history speaks loudly and clearly of their success in taking the Gospel of the Kingdom to the entire Jewish world during the first generation of the Church. With the committed work of many servants of the Lord, the task Jesus had placed on His disciples as the stipulation was accomplished during their lifetime.

Recognizing and understanding the wedding feast chronology is not only one of the most important keys to properly interpreting the significance and fulfillment of the stipulation which the Lord gave in the Olivet Discourse, but is also, in fact, one of the main keys to fully understanding the chronological order of the whole New Testament. First the Jewish Mission ends with the destruction of Jerusalem and the Temple, afterwards the Gentile Mission begins—the mission to the nations which will not end until the whole earth is filled with His glory.

In the parable of the wedding feast, Jesus laid out the requirement for the Gospel of the Kingdom being offered to the Jewish nation before judgment would fall upon Jerusalem.

Before these men would finish going through the cities of Israel, the Messianic Kingdom would be established in His resurrection, ascension and the outpouring of the Holy Spirit. Moreover, some of these same disciples would see Him coming in clouds of judgment, destroying the city of Jerusalem and its Temple. In the district of Caesarea Philippi He indisputably announced:

> "For the Son of Man is going to come in the glory of
> His Father with His angels; and will then recompense
> every man according to his deeds. Truly I say to you,
> there are some of those who are standing here who
> shall not taste death until they see the Son of Man
> coming in His kingdom." (Matthew 16:27-28)

The disciples believed Jesus was commissioning them, giving them the stipulation which was to be fulfilled during their lifetime. It is obvious from their reaction that the disciples understood and accepted Jesus' challenge. History validates their success in taking the single Gospel of the Kingdom to the entire Jewish world during the first generation of the Church. According to DeMar:

"It appears from the most credible records, that the gospel was preached in Idumea, Syria, and Mesopotamia, by Jude; in Egypt, Marmorica, Mauritania, and other parts of Africa, by Mark, Simon, and Jude; in Ethiopia, by Candace's Eunuch and Matthias; in Pontus, Galatia, and neighboring parts of Asia, by Peter; in territories of the seven Asiatic churches, by John; in Parthia, by Matthew; in Scythia, by Philip and Andrew; in the northern and western parts of Asia, by Bartholomew; in Persia, by Simon and Jude; in Media, Carmania, and several eastern parts, by Thomas; through the vast tract of Jerusalem round about Illyricum, by Paul, as also in Italy, and probably Spain, Gaul, and Britain; in most of which places Christian churches were planted, in less than thirty years after the death of Christ, which was before the destruction of Jerusalem."[1]

The Book of Acts is the history of the early Church's mission of inviting the Jews to the King's banquet. They offered their generation of Israelites peace, an escape from the coming judgment and a place in the Kingdom. The disciples preached to the Jews, calling out of the apostate nation a remnant of believers. Peter's sermon at Pentecost was pure Gospel of the Kingdom:

"This Jesus God raised up again, to which we are all witnesses. Therefore having been exalted to the right hand of God, and having received from the Father the promise of the Holy Spirit, He has poured forth that which you both see and hear...

Therefore let all the house of Israel know for certain that God has made Him both Lord and Christ—this Jesus whom you crucified." (Acts 2:32-36)

---

[1] Scott, Explanatory Notes, Practical Observations on the Holy Bible, 3:109, cited in Gary DeMar, Last Days Madness: The Folly of Trying to Predict When Christ Will Return, (Brentwood, TN: Wolgemuth and Hyatt, 1991), pp. 54-55.

Peter took his stand on the day of Pentecost and preached the first Christian sermon—the Gospel of the Kingdom to:

"...Jews living in Jerusalem, devout men, from every nation under heaven." (Acts 2:5)

In that single sermon, Peter preached to every nation under heaven where Jews had been scattered. Yet, no offer of a physical Kingdom was made. Instead, Peter preached the Gospel of the Kingdom—the Gospel of Salvation. Repeatedly, Peter made the focus of the message of Pentecost directed first to the Jews:

"Men of Judea, and all who live in Jerusalem, let this be known to you, and give heed to my words...this is what was spoken through the prophet Joel..."

"Men of Israel listen to these words..."

"My brothers may I confidently say to you..."

"Therefore let all the house of Israel know for certain that God has made Him both Lord and Christ—this Jesus whom you crucified." (Acts 2:14-36)

Peter declared in no uncertain terms that Jesus had been installed as King by God the Father. He was both Lord and Christ! The prophecies had been fulfilled. He offered as proof of his message the mighty outpouring of the Holy Spirit which had come upon the waiting body of Apostles and the inner core of Jesus' disciples who were gathered together in the upper room on the day of Pentecost. Now, the Gospel of the Kingdom was being offered in order to gather the believing remnant of Jews out of the nation before its judgment would come. As he brought his message at Pentecost to a climactic close Peter commanded his listeners:

"Be saved from this perverse generation!" (Acts 2:40)

Believing prophecy had been fulfilled and the Kingdom had been established, three thousand received Jesus as Lord in one single day!

Following Pentecost, the disciples of the Lord Jesus fully believed they were living in the age of the Spirit. They depended upon the power of the Holy Spirit. Daily the disciples went to the Temple. There they preached, reasoned and testified of the power and authority of Jesus. They were fulfilling the Jewish Mission which Jesus had given them.

Peter and John were in the Temple. There they healed a lame man. As the miracle drew a crowd, Peter began to preach:

"Men of Israel, why do you marvel at this...as if by our own power we made him walk...

The God of Abraham, Isaac, and Jacob, the God of our fathers, has glorified His servant Jesus...and raised Him from the dead.

...it is the name of Jesus which has strengthened this man, whom you see and know; and the faith which comes through Him has given him this perfect health in the presence of you all...

Repent therefore and return, that your sins may be wiped away, in order that times of refreshing may come from the presence of the Lord...

For you first, God raised up His Servant, and sent Him to bless you by turning every one of you from your wicked ways." (Acts 3:12-26)

The disciples saw their mission as fulfilling the prophetic promise to re-gather scattered Israel. The Prophet Isaiah had promised:

"Then a shoot will spring forth out of Jesse...
And the Spirit of the Lord will rest on Him...
Then it will happen on that day that the Lord
Will again recover the second time with His hand
The remnant of His people...
He will lift up a standard for the nations,
And will assemble the banished ones of Israel,
And will gather the dispersed of Judah
From the four corners of the earth." (Isaiah 10:1-12)

In the mind of the apostolic leadership of the early Church, they were gathering the dispersed by preaching the Gospel of the Kingdom and establishing the Church of Jesus Christ—the true holy nation. The Apostle James, the natural brother of Jesus, addressed the Church as:

"...the twelve tribes dispersed abroad..." (James 1:1)

James clearly equated the Church—made up, as it was initially, of the believing remnant—with the new Israel.

Peter expanded upon the understanding of James. Peter insisted the Church was the twelve scattered tribes who were being re-gathered into a holy nation in fulfillment of the Old Testament prophecies. He greeted the Church as:

"...those who reside as aliens, scattered throughout
Pontus, Galatia, Cappadocia, Asia, and Bithynia, who
are chosen according to the foreknowledge of God
the Father, by the sanctifying work of the Spirit, that
you may obey Jesus Christ..." (1 Peter 1:1-2)

Then the great Apostle made a remarkable statement. Not only was the Church to be understood as the scattered twelve tribes, but every Old Testament promise of the re-gathering of Israel was fulfilled by the forming of the believing remnant into the Church of Jesus Christ. There was not a promise of some future gathering of the nation Israel back into the land of Palestine—the prophets had seen the gathering of the Jewish believing remnant—the prophets had seen salvation!

> "As to this salvation, the prophets who prophesied of the grace that would come to you made a careful search and inquiry, seeking to know what person or time the Spirit of Christ within them was indicating as He predicted the sufferings of Christ and the glories to follow...

The Apostle carefully continues:

> "It was revealed to them [to the prophets] that they were not serving themselves, but you...

Peter was speaking to the Church!

> "in these things which now have been announced to you through those who preached the gospel to you by the Holy Spirit sent from heaven—things into which angels long to look." (1 Peter 1:10-12)

These words of the Apostle Peter to the believing Jewish remnant were received with overwhelming joy. They were experiencing what the prophets and angels had so longed to see—they were living it!

Peter proceeded. Because of the power of the Gospel of the Kingdom which they had received, they were prophetically promised a house which the Son of David would build for God the Father. God had promised David:

> "I will raise up your descendant after you, who will come forth from you, and I will establish His king-

dom. He shall build a house for My name, and I will establish His kingdom." (2 Samuel 7:12-13)

Peter taught this was no ordinary house. It was made with living stones:

> "You also, as living stones, are being built up as a spiritual house for a holy priesthood, to offer up spiritual sacrifices acceptable to God through Jesus Christ." (1 Peter 2:5)

The Church was the new Temple of God made with living stones, but there was more. Speaking to the Church, Peter demanded:

> "You are a chosen race, a royal priesthood, a holy nation, a people for God's own possession...for you were once not a people, but now you are the people of God..." (1 Peter 2:9-10)

Little wonder the early Church saw the Gospel of the Kingdom as the power of God unto salvation. They had been redeemed. They had been brought out of darkness, by the one greater than Moses, regenerated, raised up into the heavenlies, re-gathered and formed into the new holy nation, the new Israel of God, the nation producing the fruit of the Kingdom. It was this powerful Gospel of the Kingdom which the Lord Jesus had commanded His followers to take to every Jew scattered throughout the nations of the Roman Empire. The servants of Jesus did just that. Before their lives were completed, the Gospel of the Kingdom had been preached to every Jew scattered throughout the Roman world. The Jewish Mission was fulfilled in their lifetime just as Jesus had stipulated.

It was the Apostle Paul who made repeated declarations to that fact:

"First, I thank God for you all, because your faith is
being proclaimed throughout the whole world."
(Romans 1:8)

"...the gospel which has come to you, just as in all
the world also it is bearing fruit and increasing..."
(Colossians 1:5-6)

"...the gospel...which was proclaimed in all creation
under heaven." (Colossians 1:23)

Paul preached throughout most of the Roman Empire
himself. Even though he was the Apostle to the Gentiles he
recognized the stipulation which Jesus had placed on His followers. Everywhere Paul traveled to take the Gospel of the
Kingdom he followed the Lord's pattern: first to the Jew.
Immediately upon arriving in a city, Paul would go to the synagogue or meet privately with the Jewish leaders of the city in
order to convert them to Jesus as the Christ. On one occasion
Paul and his companions had come to the city of Pisidian
Antioch and:

"...on the Sabbath day they went to the synagogue
and sat down.

...Paul stood up and said, Men of Israel...listen..."
(Acts 13:14-16)

At which point Paul began an extensive message authenti-
cating the Messiahship of Jesus based upon the Old
Testament prophets, and the Lord's resurrection from the
dead. Paul continued:

"...according to promise, God has brought to Israel a
Savior, Jesus...

Brethren, sons of Abraham's family, and those who
fear God, to us the word of this salvation is sent out.

> Therefore let it be known to you, brethren, that through Him forgiveness of sins is proclaimed to you." (Acts 13:23-38)

The pattern, to the Jew first, was repeated throughout Paul's ministry:

> "...in Iconium they entered the synagogue of Jews..." (Acts 14:1)

> "...they came to Thessalonica, where there was a synagogue of the Jews. And according to Paul's custom, he went to them, and for three Sabbaths reasoned with them from the Scriptures, explaining and giving evidence that the Christ had to suffer and rise again from the dead, and saying, 'This Jesus whom I am proclaiming to you is the Christ.'" (Acts 17:1-3)

> "Paul and Silas went away by night to Berea; and when they arrived, they went into the synagogue to the Jews." (Acts 17:10)

> "...at Athens...he was reasoning in the synagogue with the Jews..." (Acts 17:17)

> "...Corinth...he was reasoning in the synagogue every Sabbath..." (Acts 18:4)

> "They came to Ephesus...Now he himself entered the synagogue and reasoned with the Jews." (Acts 18:19)

> "...Ephesus...he entered the synagogue and continued speaking out boldly for three months, reasoning and persuading them about the kingdom of God." (Acts 19:8)

Even Paul's enemies admit to his success at going first to the Jews:

> "For we have found this man a real pest and a fellow who stirs up dissension among all the Jews through-out the world, and a ringleader of the sect of the Nazarenes." (Acts 24:5)

Around A.D. 65, one year before the beginning of the siege of Jerusalem by the Roman Prince Titus, Paul the Apostle was in Rome. The Jewish leaders of the city were intrigued by his presence and agreed to meet with him. Paul followed the apostolic pattern of the early Church by taking the Gospel "first to the Jews:"

> "When we entered Rome, Paul was allowed to stay by himself, with the soldier who was guarding him. And it happened that after three days he called together those who were the leading men of the Jews..."
> (Acts 28:16-17)

> "And when they had set a day for him, they came to him at his lodging in large numbers; and he was explaining to them by solemnly testifying about the kingdom of God, and trying to persuade them con-cerning Jesus, from both the Law of Moses and from the Prophets, from morning until evening."
> (Acts 28:23)

Remember, He was confronting Jewish leaders. He was fulfill-ing the Jewish evangelistic mission:

> "They disagreed among themselves and began to leave after Paul had made this final statement, 'The Holy Spirit spoke the truth to your forefathers when he said through Isaiah the prophet, 'Go to this peo-ple and say you will be ever hearing but never under-

standing, you will be ever seeing, but never perceiving. For this people's heart has become callused, they hardly hear with their ears. They have closed their eyes. Otherwise they might see with their eyes, hear with their ears, understand with their hearts, and turn and I would heal them.'" (Acts 28:25-27)

When the Jewish leaders heard the Gospel of the Kingdom and refused the command of salvation, Paul declared:

"Therefore, I want you to know that God's salvation has been sent to the Gentiles, and they will listen." (Acts 28:28)

The apostate nation rejected the Gospel of the Kingdom. Not because they had not heard–for they had heard indeed. In fact, it was Paul who directly asserted the Gospel was taken to the hearing of every Jew during his lifetime:

"But I say, surely they [the Jews] have not heard, have they? Indeed they have; 'Their voice [of the servants of the Lord] has gone out into all the earth, and their words to the ends of the world.'" (Romans 10:18)

Clearly, the stipulation was fulfilled. With the preaching of the Gospel of the Kingdom throughout the Jewish world, the elect were gathered into the believing remnant and formed the foundation of the Church. However, the majority of the Jewish nation refused to repent and receive Jesus as Lord. Instead, they rebelled against their God and killed His servants exactly as Jesus had warned in His parable:

"But, they paid no attention and went off, one to his field, another to his business. The rest seized his servants, mistreated them and killed them." (Matthew 22:6)

His servants would undergo tremendous persecution at the hand of the Jews. Some would be killed:

"Then you will be handed over to be persecuted and put to death, and you will be hated by all nations because of me." (Matthew 24:9)

However, in the parable, those who refused to come to the banquet and those who persecuted the King's servants were to be severely judged:

"The king was enraged. He sent his army and destroyed those murderers and burned their city." (Matthew 22:7)

The King burned their city!

This was the Olivet Discourse in the form of a parable. Jesus used the parable to promise the end of Jerusalem following their refusal of His salvation invitation.

"This Gospel of the Kingdom shall be preached in the whole world for a witness to all the nations, and then the end will come." (Matthew 24:14)

Before the burning of the old city in A.D. 70, the stipulation the Lord had placed upon His disciples had been completed. The Gospel of the Kingdom was preached to the Jews scattered across the Roman Empire producing the new city, the new Jerusalem—the Church of Jesus Christ. Judgment could begin!

5

THE SIGN

The Lord had carefully maneuvered the disciples through the spurious signs and the stipulation in order to deal with their original question:

"Tell us, when will these things be, what will be the sign of Your coming, and of the end of the age?" (Matthew 24:3)

The disciples were on the Mount of Olives hearing the one they believed to be the Messiah prophesy to them that Jerusalem was about to be destroyed and its magnificent Temple torn apart stone by stone. They knew the destruction of the city was somehow related to the coming of Jesus' Messianic Kingdom, but how and when they were not certain. Following Him step by step through His explanation, they demanded to know every detail. When would these things take place? What would be the sign they were about to happen? When would Jesus come in power and glory as Messiah and what would be the sign of His Messianic Kingdom? If they were connected—how? These were critical questions.

Jesus purposefully continued His explanation:

"Therefore, when you see..." (Matthew 24:15)

He was speaking directly to His primary disciples, the inner core of the first followers of the Messiah, Peter, James, John and Andrew:

"...when you see the abomination of desolation
which was spoken of through the prophet Daniel,
standing in the holy place..." (Matthew 24:15-16)

These disciples immediately recognized the Old Testament reference Jesus used. The Abomination of Desolation was a passage which every Jewish boy had heard since his youth. The great Prophet Daniel had promised an Abomination of Desolation in which the "people of the prince" would come and destroy the city of Jerusalem following the death of the Messiah:

"Messiah will be cut off and have nothing, and
[after Messiah's death] the people of the prince who
is to come will destroy the city and the sanctuary...on the wing of abominations will come one
who makes desolate, even until a complete destruction, one that is decreed, is poured out on the one
who makes desolate." (Daniel 9:26-27)

Jesus connected the Abomination of Desolation with the coming of His Messianic Kingdom. Yet how would the Abomination of Desolation be a sign to the disciples?

"...when you see the abomination of
desolation...THEN..." (Matthew 24:15-16)

Confusion rushed across their faces.

Jesus took another approach. He interpreted Daniel's prophecy to make His instruction as clear as possible. He said to His disciples standing before Him that day:

> "When you see Jerusalem surrounded by armies, then recognize that her desolation is at hand."
> (Luke 21:20)

Jesus interpreted Daniel! When Jerusalem becomes surrounded by armies—that would be the Abomination of Desolation. Hearing the Lord's explanation was overwhelming. They were about to experience the Abomination of Desolation. They looked at one another in disbelief. Could this be real? How would they survive? What would happen to their families? Would this be the end of their lives?

Deliberately, painstakingly, weighing every word to make His explanation clear, the Lord gave them explicit instructions which would ultimately save their lives. Instructions they obeyed!

> "...When you see the Abomination of Desolation...let those in Judea flee to the mountains."

> "...let him who is on the housetop not come down to get the things out that are in his house."

> "...let him who is in the field not turn back to get his cloak."

> "...woe to those who are with child and to those who nurse babes in those days."

> "...pray that your flight be not in the winter, or on a Sabbath." (Matthew 24:16-20)

This was not a Messianic diatribe preparing some future generation to survive a future tribulation. Jesus was speaking directly to these disciples on the Mount of Olives concerning events which would take place during their lifetime. Events which would precede the sign of the Kingdom. Events which would signal the end of the Old Covenant nation. Events which would be so filled with danger, these very disciples and their families would be forced to flee for their lives—and they did!

The Lord continued:

"Then there will be a great tribulation..."

Then—during the lives of these very disciples!

"...there will be a great tribulation, such as has not occurred since the beginning of the world until now, nor ever shall." (Matthew 24:21)

The Lord's teaching was clear and dramatic. The circumstances surrounding the Abomination of Desolation would be so severe that nothing in the history of the world would compare. In fact, it would be so intensely horrific it would threaten to destroy all Jewish life:

"And unless those days had been cut short, no life would have been saved..." (Matthew 24:22)[1]

Answering the disciples' question, the Lord unveiled His eschatology of the Kingdom. The time of the disciples would be the time of "great tribulation" which would end with the fall of Jerusalem. The Roman army would set Jerusalem on fire and destroy both the City and its Temple. Jesus was not speaking to these men of the armies of a future Revived Roman Empire led by a future Roman Prince, or a future time

---

[1] "...But 'those days' can hardly mean anything else than the days of flight from Judea" John A. Broadus, Commentary on the Gospel of Matthew, ed. Alva Hovey, (Philadelphia: American Baptist Publication Society, 1886), p.488.

of tribulation. Clearly, He was speaking to them of the powerful armies of the Roman Empire which already existed in their day. Jesus spoke of a Roman Desolator whom some of these disciples would see with their own eyes.

The Lord unveiled to His men prophetic events which He promised would take place during their lifetime...events which were filled with eschatological importance.

Eschatology is the study of last things or endtimes. However, when the Old Testament prophets spoke of the last days or the endtimes, they were not speaking of the end of the modern world or the material universe. Instead they were speaking of the last days of the age of Moses—the end of the Old Covenant era. They were also prophesying the dawning of Messiah's day—the inauguration of the New Covenant era.

In His Olivet discourse Jesus was absolutely faithful to the eschatology of the Old Testament prophets. As He shared with His disciples on the Mount of Olives, Jesus unfolded for them the true meaning of these eschatological prophecies. The fall of Jerusalem and the destruction of the magnificent Temple of Herod would fulfill the terrible judgments of God which had been foretold by the prophets—the "days of vengeance" prophesied by Moses and Isaiah.

Imagine their shock as the disciples realized they and their families were living in the last days. Their generation would be the last generation of the Old Covenant era.

Jewish historian Josephus describes in graphic detail the horrendous events which took place during the destruction of Israel by the armies of Rome. He writes of a progressive national insanity resulting in the inability to reason, frenzied mobs attacking one another, the crazed and desperate search for food, mass murders, suicides, executions, and families cannibalizing one another.

"The city was divided into armies encamped against one another, and the preservation of the one party was in the destruction of the other; so the day-time was spent in the shedding of blood, and the night in fear."[2]

Historian Joseph Carrington agrees:

"While Titus was besieging it from without, the three leaders of rival factions were fighting fiercely within: but for this the city might have staved off defeat for a long time, even perhaps indefinitely, for no great army could support itself long in those days in the neighborhood of Jerusalem; there was no water and no supplies."[3]

During the Roman siege of Jerusalem the city's supplies began to dwindle. The inhabitants of Jerusalem went through incredible suffering. What the Jews did to themselves as they divided into factions and fought within the city was far more barbarous and devastating than what the Romans did to them when the city of Jerusalem finally fell. Josephus observes:

"It was then common to see the city filled with dead bodies, still lying unburied, and those of old men, mixed with infants, all dead, and scattered about together; women also lay amongst them, without any covering for their nakedness..."[4]

As the city ran out of food and supplies the people fought among themselves for the crumbs. Chilton describes the time:

"For, since nowhere was grain to be seen, men would break into houses, and if they found some they mis-

---

[2] Flavius Josephus, "The Wars of the Jews," in The Complete Works of Josephus, pp. 429-605, tr. William Whiston, (Grand Rapids: Kregel, 1981), II.XVIII.2, 493.
[3] Philip Carrington, The Meaning of the Revelation, (London: SPCK, 1931), p. 266.
[4] Josephus, "Wars," II.XVIII.2, p. 493.

treated the occupants for having denied their possession of it; if they found none they tortured them as
if they had concealed it more carefully. Proof
whether they had food or not was provided by the
physical appearance of the wretches; those still in
good condition were deemed to be well provided
with food, while those who were already wasting
away were passed over, for it seemed pointless to kill
persons who would soon die of starvation. Many
secretly bartered their possessions for a single measure of wheat if they happened to be rich, barley if
they were poor. Then they shut themselves up in the
darkest corners of their houses; in extremity of
hunger some even ate their grain underground, while
others baked it, guided by necessity and fear.
Nowhere was a table laid— the food was snatched
half-cooked from the fire and torn into pieces."[5]

During the tribulation leading to the fall of Jerusalem in
A.D. 70, Josephus tells of Jewish mothers who boiled their
children and ate the flesh. The city was totally cut off from
outside support and was being torn apart by warring factions
internally. Carrington writes:

"This fighting within the city delivered it quickly into
the hands of Titus; 'the days were shortened.' "[6]

As Jesus had promised, heaven intervened in order to save
the infant Church:

"...but for the sake of the elect those days shall be
cut short...Behold, I have told you in advance."
(Matthew 24:22,25)

[5] Chilton, Days of Vengeance, p. 190.
[6] Carrington, p. 266.

The Lord had answered the first part of the disciples' question:

"When will these things be..." (Matthew 24:3)

Jesus was definite. The events, which would ultimately end with the destruction of Jerusalem, would begin with the greatest tribulation the world would ever experience as the city would be surrounded by the armies of the Roman Empire—the Abomination of Desolation. That tribulation would result in the destruction of Jerusalem—the end of apostate Israel—the sign of the Kingdom.

However, there was more to the disciples' question. Not only did they ask when, they also wanted to know what would be the sign:

"...what would be the sign of your coming and the end of the age?" (Matthew 24:3)

The revelation which Jesus opened to these disciples stretched them to their limits. Those final days of the Lord's physical life had been a whirlwind of conflicts and questions. Yet, as a result of those moments with Jesus the disciples were more convinced than ever of His Messianic authority and authenticity. He had taken the greatest prophets of the Old Testament and used them to prove His Messianic claim. Then, He had systematically laid before the disciples their role in fulfilling the most important events in history. Finally, the Lord Jesus answered their question:

"Immediately after the tribulation of those days the sun will be darkened, and the moon will not give its light, and the stars will fall from the sky, and the powers of the heavens will be shaken..."
(Matthew 24:29)

The Lord confidently presented the sign of the Kingdom to His disciples with a plethora of prophetic terminology spoken by the Old Testament prophets describing the judgment of God in their day. His strategy was critical. Drawing upon the Prophet's description of His Father's former dealings with the nations to describe the operation of His own Kingdom, Jesus quoted Isaiah to present the sign of His coming Kingdom.

The great Prophet had described the judgment of God the Father upon the Kingdom of Babylon with what seemed to be end-of-the-world terminology. Now, Jesus used the same language to answer the disciples' question regarding the sign of the Kingdom.

Contrary to what some believe, He was not speaking of the end of the world when He spoke of a darkened sun, a moon with no light, stars falling from the sky, and powers of heaven being shaken. Nor was He speaking of His second advent prior to the establishment of an imagined, earthly, political, Jewish, millennial Kingdom. Jesus was speaking of the sign of His present heavenly Kingdom—His judgment coming in the power and glory of His Messianic Kingdom to judge unrighteous men and nations based on their response to the Gospel of the Kingdom—beginning with Israel, the apostate nation.

Isaiah had used these identical words to describe the previous judgment of God the Father against the unrighteousness of the Babylonian Kingdom in the time of the Old Testament era:

"The oracle concerning Babylon...
Behold, the day of the Lord is coming,
Cruel, with fury and burning anger,
To make the land a desolation;
And He will exterminate its sinners from it.

For the stars of heaven and their constellations
Will not flash forth their light;
The sun will be dark when it rises,
And the moon will not shed its light...
Therefore I shall make the heavens tremble,
And the earth will be shaken from its place
At the fury of the Lord of hosts
In the day of His burning anger..."

"Behold, I am going to stir up the Medes
against them..." (Isaiah 13:1, 9-17)

The coming of the day of the Lord, with the stars falling from their constellations, the sun and the moon darkened, the earth shaken from its place, *sounds like the end of the world!* But Isaiah was not prophesying the end of history and the material universe, nor the Second Coming. He was prophesying the end of the Babylonian Empire which actually took place in the time of the Prophet Daniel.

This was an *end-of-a-civilization* prophecy. This was an *end-of-a-culture* prophecy.

God's wrath was coming upon Babylon. God did not come bodily. He did not come merely in a spiritual judgment, but He did come. Because of their injustice, oppression and violence the Lord spoke through His Prophet to warn Babylon, the wicked nation, that He would come in judgment and establish justice. When the judgment of God came, He sent the armies of the Medes and the Persians as the instrument of His judgment against the Kingdom of Babylon. The sign on the earth of the Father's heavenly reign over His creation was prophetically seen in His judgment of Babylon by the Medes.

In the highly symbolic and picturesque phrases, "the day of the Lord," "the stars of heaven will not flash their light," "the sun will be dark," "the moon will not shed its light," "the heavens tremble," and "the earth will be shaken from its place," Isaiah used Old Testament poetic language—graphic terminology, which Chilton has rightly called "collapsing universe" terminology—to represent the full impact of God's wrath on the Babylonian culture.

It was "lights out" and the end of the world for Babylon.

God the Father was ruling and administrating the Kingdom of Heaven under the Old Covenant. He was ruling history, judging nations and establishing righteousness.

These passages of Isaiah were critical to understanding Jesus on the Mount of Olives. Isaiah continued:

> "...that you will take up this taunt against the *king of Babylon*, and say...
> 'How you have fallen from heaven,
> O star of the morning, son of the dawn...
> Those who see you will gaze at you,
> they will ponder over you, saying,
> 'Is this *the man* who made the earth tremble,
> Who shook kingdoms,
> Who made the world like a wilderness
> And overthrew its cities,
> Who did not allow his prisoners to go home?"
> (Isaiah 14:4, 12, 16, 17)

The Prophet Isaiah prophesied the overthrow of the king of Babylon by the judgment of God. Isaiah spoke of the Babylonian king as a star of the morning—*the man who made the earth tremble.* When the Babylonian kingdom was overthrown the Prophet saw the sun blackened, the moon withholding its light and the stars falling. Isaiah was speaking of God the Father's destruction of the Babylonian kingdom.

Jesus used this identical language to speak of His destruction of Israel.

Standing before His disciples on the Mount of Olives, Jesus reached back to the Old Testament. Using Old Testament poetic language which described the government of God as it functioned in the days of the kingdom of Babylon, Jesus described the coming of His Messianic Kingdom. As God the Father administrated the Kingdom of Heaven under the Old Covenant, so Jesus, the Son of God, would administrate the Kingdom of Heaven under the New Covenant. Judgment against the enemies of His Messianic Kingdom would be described in terms of:

"...the sun will be darkened, the moon will not give its light, the stars will fall from the sky..."
(Matthew 24:29)

In the Olivet Discourse, Jesus purposefully co-mingled two distinct Old Testament prophetic occurrences in order to answer His disciples' question concerning the sign of His Kingdom. First, He used the Abomination of Desolation spoken by Daniel. Its ultimate meaning was clear. The armies of Rome would surround Jerusalem; the Harlot-city and its Temple would be destroyed! Second, He used the Prophet's poetic language which described the judgment of God the Father on the kingdom of Babylon to describe His own judgment upon His enemies, beginning with the apostate nation. In doing so, Jesus was stating in the strongest possible biblical language that the destruction of Jerusalem at the hands of the Roman armies would come as a direct judgment from His Messianic Kingdom and would be *the sign on earth to all the nations of the world throughout history that the Son of Man is ruling in heaven.*

Jesus did not invent the terminology He used on the Mount of Olives. Neither was it new language to these men. He used Old Testament language to communicate with them. He did so to make certain they understood that the Old

Testament Messianic prophecies were being fulfilled in His life and ministry. He was the one whom the prophets had promised!

Remember, when the Prophet Isaiah spoke, his language seemed to be speaking of the end of the world. However, it was not! His terminology described the end of a particular nation. His language described actual historic events which took place in the time of the Prophet Daniel. Climaxing in the fall of Babylon, those events changed the world! That catastrophic and historic fall was a sign to the nations that Jehovah ruled in the heavens.

Standing on the Mount of Olives with these original Apostles overlooking the ancient city and its Temple, Jesus prophesied the sign of His Kingdom—the destruction of Jerusalem and the Temple. Some of His twelve disciples would live to experience apostate Israel being judged by His heavenly judgment. Jesus described the judgment as:

> "...the sun will be darkened, the moon will not give
> its light, and the stars will fall from the heavens."
> (Matthew 24:29)

Jesus prophetically saw the end of Old Covenant Israel. Its destruction would take place as a direct judgment from King Jesus in heaven. Seated upon the throne of His Messianic Kingdom, the Lord Jesus withdrew heaven's protection from the apostate nation and Harlot-city. Opening the sulfurous pit of hell and permitting the total demonization of the nation, He at last gathered His armies from across the Roman Empire to surround, besiege and raze the city with its already spiritually desolate Temple. He was "coming on the glory-clouds of Heaven," "judging and making war" upon His enemies who having willfully rejected His offer of mercy and grace and who, trampling under feet His precious blood of the New Covenant, resisted the ministry of the Holy Spirit through His apostolic messengers. As "the smoke of their torment" ascended to heaven the sun would be darkened, the moon would not give its light and the stars would fall from the heavens—the Kingdom would be taken from the apostates and be given to the New Testament Saints.

As the apostate nation was judged, its leaders killed, its city burned, its Temple decimated, its stones torn apart, the sign of the Kingdom would be revealed. The nations of the world would see the destruction of Jerusalem—the sign on the earth that Jesus was reigning in heaven as King of Kings and Lord of Lords.

"Then shall appear the sign of the Son of Man in heaven." (Matthew 24:30 KJV)

The sign occurred in A.D. 70!

6

THE SEASON OF THE SIGN

He was not vague. He used no subtleties. Instead, Jesus was direct, precise, and extremely explicit. Not only did He desire the disciples to know, He demanded it! They were living in the generation which would experience the coming of His Messianic Kingdom, and its attendant judgment upon Israel. He stated it with the greatest clarity. In fact, there was nothing in His earthly ministry with which He was more precise than the defining and timing of the sign of His Kingdom.

Earlier that day the disciples had heard Jesus as He confronted the religious hierarchy of Israel face to face. Standing before the apostate leaders of the nation He loved, He brought His prophetic litany of judgment to a climactic conclusion by declaring:

> "Truly I say unto you, (speaking directly to the leaders of Israel) all these things shall come upon *this generation!*" (Matthew 23:36)

The destruction of Jerusalem, which would be the sign on the earth of the reign of Jesus in heaven as King of Kings, would take place during the lifetime of these specific leaders— *their generation.*

Ultimately, even the length of a single generation was too vague for Jesus. Zeroing in on the timing of the sign, the Lord gave the disciples two precise indicators. The season of the sign would be the time between two specific events.

The first indicator was the siege of Jerusalem:

"When you see Jerusalem surrounded by armies, then recognize her desolation is at hand." (Luke 21:20)

Once again, the destruction of Jerusalem was the key. When the disciples saw the city surrounded by armies...the season of the sign had begun.

The second indicator was simple. The length of the disciples' generation:

"Truly I say to you, *this generation* (the disciples' generation) will not pass away until all these things take place." (Matthew 24:34)

The sign of the Kingdom would occur before the generation of the disciples ended. Jesus had narrowed the season. The season of the sign of the Kingdom would begin with the siege of Jerusalem and end with the close of the disciples' generation.

Peter, James, John, Andrew and the other disciples heard exactly what Jesus said. He spoke of their generation. Or, as He put it, "this generation." If He had been thinking of a future generation he would have said—"that generation." But, He did not do so.

Jesus had spoken many times of "this generation." In every instance the Lord was speaking of the generation in which He and His disciples lived. The same was true as He stood on the Mount of Olives overlooking the city which He would soon destroy. Jesus insisted His own twelve disciples fully understand that the sign of His Kingdom would occur during their lives...their generation. Some of the twelve would be alive during the season of the sign.

It is critical to comprehend the strategy of Jesus. From the very outset of His ministry the Lord had prepared His disciples to expect His Messianic Kingdom during their lives. As He called them to follow Him, He did so declaring the Kingdom was imminent. His first public message which initially drew them to Him was filled with expectation of the Kingdom:

"The time is fulfilled, and the kingdom of heaven is *at hand*; repent and believe the gospel." (Mark 1:15)

Responding to Jesus' explicit declaration of the nearness of the Kingdom, the disciples left everything to follow Him:

"He said to them, 'Follow me and I will make you fishers of men.' And immediately they left their nets and followed Him." (Matthew 4:19-20)

They followed fully anticipating they would see the Messianic Kingdom during their lives. They would not be disappointed! Everywhere Jesus went, His preaching was replete with the promise and power of the Kingdom:

"Jesus was going about in all Galilee, teaching in their synagogues, and proclaiming *the gospel of the kingdom*, and healing every kind of disease and every kind of sickness among the people." (Matthew 4:23)

Initially, the disciples wanted to keep the Lord to themselves in Capernaum. Yet, the drive within Jesus to preach the Gospel of the Kingdom consumed Him. He saw it as the pure purpose of His earthly ministry:

"I must preach the kingdom of God to the other
cities also, for I was sent for this purpose."
(Luke 4:43)

Before leaving the beautiful seaside city of Capernaum, Jesus called His disciples up the graceful mountain side and taught them. All of His teaching was filled with the expectation and blessings of the Kingdom:

"Blessed are the poor in spirit, *for theirs is the kingdom of heaven*. Blessed are those who mourn... Blessed are the gentle... Blessed are those who hunger and thirst for righteousness... Blessed are the merciful...Blessed are the pure in heart... Blessed are the peacemakers... Blessed are those who have been persecuted for the sake of righteousness, *for theirs is the kingdom of heaven*." (Matthew 5:2-10)

Jesus encapsulated the promised blessings of the Kingdom with the expectation of the Kingdom.

One of the most remarkable examples of the Lord teaching the nearness of the Kingdom to his disciples was His instruction regarding prayer. The daily prayer of His disciples was to include a single line filled with the expectancy of the Kingdom:

"Thy kingdom come..." (Matthew 6:10)

"Thy kingdom come" was their faith. Jesus directed them to pray believing God would answer their prayer, and as a result, they fully anticipated their prayer for the coming Kingdom to be fulfilled during their lives.

Later, the Lord summoned His disciples:

"He gave them authority over unclean spirits, to cast them out, and to heal every kind of disease and every kind of sickness." (Matthew 10:1)

Then, He instructed them:

"As you go, preach, saying, 'The kingdom of heaven is at hand.'" (Matthew 10:7)

Interestingly, Jesus gave them authority for a specific mission. They were to demonstrate the power of the Kingdom of Heaven with their authority over the spirit world. And, they were to preach with the authority of the Messiah the message of the Kingdom. That message was to be full of immediacy. They were to declare to their generation, in no uncertain terms, Messiah's Kingdom was at hand. It would be established during their lives.

As Jesus sent them out with authority to preach and perform miracles, He gave them a clear time reference for the coming of His Kingdom:

"...truly I say to you, you shall not finish going through the cities of Israel, *until the Son of Man comes.*" (Matthew 10:23)

Jesus promised His disciples that before they could finish preaching the Gospel of the Kingdom to Israel, they would live to experience the season of the sign.

The disciples were with Jesus as He preached throughout the cities of Israel. At every turn He was reassuring them of the reality of the Kingdom, promising its immediacy, and demonstrating its power. Much of that power was seen in His miracles. They were awesome. Yet, more importantly, the miracles were constant manifestations of the imminence of

Messiah's Kingdom. As He preached, He healed. As He healed, He preached. With both word and deed the disciples were experiencing first hand the authority of the soon-coming Kingdom.

What a season in which to live. The prophets of the Old Testament had only dreamed of seeing the miraculous power of Messiah. They had seen a sick nation desperately needing the healing of the Lord:

> "The whole head is sick,
> And the whole heart is faint.
> (Speaking of the nation of Israel)
> From the sole of the foot even to the head
> There is nothing sound in it,
> Only bruises, welts, and raw wounds..." (Isaiah 1:5-6)

God was sending His Messiah into a sick and rebellious nation. Yet, the Messiah was to bring healing to the regathered remnant, and build a holy nation from the outcasts and afflicted. Micah had prophesied the Lord's Day would be a time in which the Messiah would:

> "...assemble the lame,
> And gather the outcasts,
> Even those I have afflicted.
> I will make the lame a remnant,
> And the outcasts a strong nation." (Micah 4:6-7)

Every miracle Jesus performed spoke volumes to the nation. They were each an action parable promising the Kingdom was at hand. They identified Jesus as Messiah and demonstrated His Kingdom purpose. Fulfilling the prophets' promises, Jesus was the Son of God who would bring healing to the believing remnant:

"Behold My Servant, whom I uphold;
My chosen one in whom My soul delights.
I have put My Spirit upon Him...
To open blind eyes..." (Isaiah 42:1-7)

Naturally, Jesus knew He was the miracle-working Messiah of Isaiah. As He began His earthly ministry, He returned to the synagogue in Nazareth and stood to read. He opened the book of Isaiah and astounded the crowd which had filled the building:

"The Spirit of the Lord is upon Me,
Because He anointed Me to preach the gospel
to the poor.
He has sent Me to proclaim release to the captives,
And the recovery of *sight to the blind...*" (Luke 4:18)

To insure those at Nazareth did not miss the point, He boldly declared:

"Today this Scripture has been fulfilled in your
hearing." (Luke 4:21)

Every time a blind eye was opened, or a lame leg was made well, or a dumb tongue could speak it was a sign the Messiah had come to heal the nation from it spiritual sickness. The prophets were being fulfilled.

These were exceptional moments for the Lord's men, and Jesus made sure they took full advantage of them. At one point, in the midst of teaching Kingdom parables, Jesus turned to His disciples and said:

"Blessed are your eyes, because they see; and blessed
are your ears, because they hear. For truly I say to
you, that many prophets and righteous men desired
to see what you see, and did not see it; and to hear
what you hear, and did not hear it."
(Matthew 13:16-17)

Today! There was no waiting for a future generation, and there was no suggestion of a postponed fulfillment of the prophets' expectation. Messiah's Kingdom was at hand. He was not speaking to some future generation of followers. His target was His own twelve. They were living in the season of Messiah. With their own eyes they saw the miracles of the Kingdom, and with their own ears they heard the Gospel of the Kingdom. Isaiah, the great Prophet had promised a messenger of peace who would preach the Gospel of the Kingdom and usher in the Lord's day:

"How lovely on the mountains
Are the feet of him who brings good news,
Who announces peace
And brings good news of happiness,
Who announces salvation,
And says to Zion, 'Your God reigns!'" (Isaiah 52:7)

Malachi was in concert with Isaiah. He too had seen the Messenger of the New Covenant:

"The Lord whom you seek, will suddenly come to
His temple; and the messenger of the covenant, in
whom you delight, behold, He is coming..."
(Malachi 3:1)

Every Jew knew of this Messenger. Among the Jews who lived at the time of Jesus, the thought of the preacher of peace remained very much alive. As the crowds heard Jesus, the picture of Isaiah's prophesied "messenger" was in their minds. They were living in the generation which would see the Messiah's Kingdom.

Even His enemies recognized the authority and power which was on Him. His preaching and miracles made a tremendous impact on everyone who experienced them. At one point He healed a demon-possessed blind and dumb man, casting out the evil spirits. When the multitude recognized the power He controlled, they immediately began to ask if He was the Messiah:

> "All the multitude were amazed, and began to say, 'This man cannot be the Son of David, can He?'" (Matthew 12:23)

Why would the multitude make such a statement? They knew the Old Testament prophets. The Son of David was to be the deliverer of Israel. Under His shepherding care they would no longer be the prey of their enemies:

> "I will seek the lost, bring back the scattered, bind up the broken, and strengthen the sick…Therefore, I will deliver My flock, and they will no longer be a prey…I will set over them one shepherd, My servant David, and he will feed them…" (Ezekiel 34:16-23)

Every miracle of Jesus demonstrated the power of the soon-coming Messianic Kingdom. But, those who refused to accept Him as Messiah were outraged! Rather than receive His Kingdom, the Pharisees accused Jesus of operating by the power of Satan:

> "This man casts out demons only by Beelzebul the ruler of demons." (Matthew 12:24)

Jesus knew their every thought, and responded:

> "Any kingdom divided against itself is laid waste…
> If Satan casts out Satan, he is divided against himself; how then shall his kingdom stand…
> But if I cast out demons by the Spirit of God, then *the kingdom of God has come upon you.*"
> (Matthew 12:25-28)

Jesus understood His power over Satan as an absolute indication of the power and glory of His soon-coming Kingdom. He was announcing to His generation that they would live to see the season of the sign of the Kingdom.

This was not an isolated incident.

Throughout His earthly ministry Jesus was constantly waging war upon the forces of Satan. The disciples clearly saw these conflicts between the Kingdom of Heaven and the rule of Satan as proof of the authority and power of the coming Messianic Kingdom. Time and time again Jesus' entire approach in dealing with Satan was to demonstrate to His twelve the unsurpassed power of His Kingdom over the dominion of Satan.

These were critical lessons for the disciples. Jesus was equipping them for war!

Following the victorious death, resurrection, and ascension of Jesus, the Lord would baptize His followers with the Holy Spirit. The disciples would then operate in His Kingdom with the authority and power of the Holy Spirit; an authority and power which would only be available in Messiah's Kingdom. In fact, the exercise of the Lord's power over the devil and the devil's rule had the coming of the Messianic Kingdom as its foundation. If the Kingdom had not come to their generation, the disciples would have had no position from which to fight, and Satan's rule would have gone unchallenged.

Ironically, the demons themselves testified of the imminence of the Kingdom. Their response to Jesus was staggering. When Jesus confronted demons, they would cry out as in great fear. It was as though they possessed a supernatural knowledge of who He was and the purpose of His Messianic mission. At Capernaum He encountered a demon possessed man as He entered the synagogue:

"There was in their synagogue a man with an unclean spirit; and he cried out, saying, 'What do we have to do with You, Jesus of Nazareth? Have You come *to destroy us? I know who You are—the Holy One of God!*' (Mark 1:23-24)

The demons were preaching on His behalf!

How could demons have been concerned about the possibility of their destruction without knowing the certainty of His Kingdom? Obviously, they knew. Remarkable! Even the demons were expecting His Kingdom, and understood its purpose.

The Lord Jesus constantly taught His disciples to expect the Kingdom during their lives. All of His instruction was to prepare them for His Messianic reign. One of Jesus' favorite teaching techniques was the parable. He was a master at weaving the most complex theological truth into a simple story. On one occasion the disciples asked him point blank:

"Why do You speak to them in parables?" (Matthew 13:10)

His response was direct, and profound:

"To you it has been granted to know the *mysteries of the kingdom*, but to them it has not been granted." (Matthew 13:11)

These twelve incredible individuals had been granted the greatest blessing in history. They were His disciples. He loved them, and poured the truth of the Kingdom into their lives. In doing so, He readied them for the most significant challenge any group of men would ever face. They were the initial ones to take the Gospel of the Kingdom to their generation. Every miracle He performed, every word He uttered in their presence, every parable He taught them, equipped them, prepared them for their great work:

> "When anyone hears the *word of the kingdom*, and
> does not understand it, the evil one comes and
> snatches away what has been sown in his heart..."

It was that word of the Kingdom which the disciples would carry to their world. It must be correct. They must make it clear. It must be presented with power and demonstration. Satan must not be allowed to steal their work. Again and again He taught them:

> The *kingdom of heaven* may be compared to a man
> who sowed good seed in his field..."

> "The *kingdom of heaven* is like a mustard seed..."

> "The *kingdom of heaven* is like leaven..."
> (Matthew 13:19-33)

Explicit in every parable was the truth of the soon-coming Kingdom. The Kingdom and its attendant Gospel would be the sole content of their message to their generation. When they failed to fully grasp His teachings He would take them aside to explain. It was essential for them to understand:

> "The disciples came to Him saying, 'Explain to us
> the parable of the tares of the field.' And He
> answered and said, 'The one who sows the good seed
> is the Son of Man (the Messiah), the field is the
> world; and as for the good seed, these are the *sons of
> the kingdom*...'"

> "The Son of Man will send forth His angels, and
> they will gather out of His kingdom all stumbling
> blocks..."

"Then the righteous will shine forth as the sun in *the kingdom*..." (Matthew 13:36-43)

Detail after detail after detail...all surrounding the truth of the Kingdom...truth which His twelve disciples would need during their generation.

"The *kingdom of heaven* is like a treasure hidden in a field..."

"The *kingdom of heaven* is like a merchant seeking fine pearls..."

"The *kingdom of heaven* is like a dragnet..."

"Therefore every scribe who has become a *disciple of the kingdom* of heaven is like a head of a household, who brings forth out of his treasure things new and old." (Matthew 13:44-52)

As Jesus further prepared His twelve, He gave them one last test to pass at Caesarea Philippi. It was there that Simon Peter boldly passed the test by declaring:

"Thou art the Christ, the Son of the living God." (Matthew 16:16)

Peter understood. Jesus was the Christ! Jesus proudly responded:

"Blessed are you, Simon Barjona, because flesh and blood did not reveal this to you, but My Father who is in heaven. And I also say that you are Peter, and upon this rock I will build My church; and the gates of Hell shall not overpower it. *I will give you the keys of the kingdom of heaven*; and whatever you bind on earth shall be bound in heaven, and whatever you loose on earth shall be loosed in heaven." (Matthew 16:17-19)

Jesus made a remarkable statement. He would give the keys of the Kingdom of Heaven to Peter, one of the apostolic foundation stones of the Church. There was no word of a earthly, political, kingdom. No word of Jesus reigning over His Kingdom from earthly Jerusalem. No word of postponing the Kingdom to some future generation. The Church would possess the keys of the Kingdom—not physical Israel!

Peter was overwhelmed. Only as his ministry progressed could Peter have known all Jesus was saying. Obviously, Jesus believed Peter and the disciples would play significant roles in the Kingdom of Heaven, which would require the Kingdom to begin during their lifetime. Jesus made that requirement perfectly clear and promised it would be so. Speaking specifically to His disciples, He declares:

> "Truly I say to you, there are some of those who are standing here who shall not taste death until they see the Son of Man coming in His kingdom."
> (Matthew 16:27)

The Lord constantly drew the timing of the sign of the Kingdom more and more precisely. He was preparing and challenging His disciples. He could not have been more direct!

They would hear Him make the same statement a few days later. Only hours before giving the Olivet Discourse Jesus confronted the scribes and Pharisees...the Jewish leaders of His generation. He declared to them He is the "Chief Corner Stone" which they have rejected. Then He reminded them of the judgment of God which would follow their rejection:

"The Kingdom of God will be taken away from you,
and be given to a nation producing the fruit of it.
And he who falls on this stone will be broken to
pieces; but on whomever it falls, it will scatter
like dust." (Matthew 21:43-44)

Their reaction was certain:

"They understood He was speaking about them."
(Matthew 21:45)

Though the Pharisees hated Jesus to the point of death,
they still knew He was speaking about them. After warning
them their promised Messianic Kingdom was to be taken
away from them, and their beloved Jerusalem would be
destroyed, He pinpointed the time of the judgment:

"Truly I say to you, all these things shall come upon
this generation." (Matthew 23:36)

The Lord's judgment would come upon Jerusalem during
the generation of those specific scribes and Pharisees. They
were living in the season of the sign. That judgment would be
the sign to the disciples, to Israel, and the nations that
Messiah's Kingdom had been established.

Even during the closing hours of His life Jesus remained
insistent upon the imminence of His Kingdom. As Jesus
stood trial for His life, Caiaphus, the high priest, railed
at Jesus:

"I adjure You by the living God, that You tell us
whether You are the Christ, the Son of God."
(Matthew 26:63)

Jesus looked directly into the eyes of the High Priest. He
measured every word He was about to speak. Each word rang
with the weight of heaven:

"You have said it yourself; nevertheless I tell you,
hereafter *YOU shall see the Son of Man sitting at the right
hand of power, and coming on the clouds of heaven.*"
(Matthew 26:64)

Caiaphus was enraged! Jesus' answer had ignited the
atmosphere of the court into murderous contempt. Caiaphus
would live to see this Jesus of Nazareth sitting at the right
hand of majesty and coming in the clouds administrating the
Kingdom of God. Jesus mixed no words. He boldly told
Caiaphus and the entire packed courtroom that the High
Priest would live to see the destruction of Jerusalem. Caiaphus
stood and in a display of religious indignation, literally tear-
ing his robes, he screamed at the top of his voice:

"He has blasphemed!" (Matthew 26:65)

But, it was too late for Caiaphus and all the religious role
players of his day. They were living in the generation of the
coming of Messiah. Less than forty years later, Jesus would
send in the Roman army to destroy Jerusalem, the Temple,
the high priest, and his entire family. There was no question
left. Jesus had pinpointed the season of the sign. The siege of
Jerusalem would begin the season. It would end with the fall
of the city during the life of the disciples. Thus, the season of
the sign.

The season began in the spring of A.D. 66. In September
of A.D. 70, the sign occurred–Jerusalem was destroyed!

7

THE SIGNIFICANCE OF THE SIGN

Thunderstorms were building over the Mount of Olives that damp spring evening. As cool breezes blew across the mountain, Jesus could feel the anxiety of the disciples. Their concern was not toward the darkening clouds, but the significance of the storm of judgment which was poised against their nation. Taking advantage of the storms, Jesus reaffirmed the power of His coming in Messianic judgment against apostate Israel. The sign of His Messianic Kingdom would be inescapable. The consequence of His Kingdom upon Israel would be as powerful as a lightning bolt. As the mighty thunder which follows, His judgment would shake the foundation of the nation. Using the heavens as a great illustration, the Lord directed their attention to the gathering storm:

> "Just as the lightning comes from the east, and flashes to the west, so shall the coming of the Son of Man be." (Matthew 24:27)

His coming in judgment would be spectacular. All the world would see His display of heavenly power. As a result of His judgment of Israel, the once mighty covenantal nation would be dead in the sight of God. The disciples must expect nothing else:

"Wherever the corpse is, there the vultures will gather." (Matthew 24:28)

Every evening great birds of prey gathered over Jerusalem. That night was no exception. Attracted by the animals being slaughtered for tribal feasts and the continuous sacrifices in the Temple, the disciples could see the vultures as they danced their flights of death over the city. Jesus used the gathering birds to graphically tell His disciples the birds of prey of foreign armies would gather to take their fill upon Jerusalem before their generation ended.

The city seemed to grow larger with the coming of night. From their vantage point overlooking Jerusalem, they could see sporadic evening fires appearing across the horizon as people hurriedly prepared for the close of the day, and its impending storms. Sounds of the city rolled up the Mount of Olives as Jesus seized the moment to lead His disciples into the significance of the destruction of Jerusalem... *the significance of the sign of His Kingdom*:

"Immediately after the tribulations of those days the sun will be darkened, and the moon will not give its light, and the stars will fall from the sky..." (Matthew 24:29)

Jesus left no room for speculation. He was not speaking to some future generation of believers thousands of years removed from His disciples. The events He unfolded were for their generation. In fact, the Lord had specifically informed the disciples only moments earlier of the coming tribulation which would occur with the destruction of Jerusalem during their lives. Now, to His own twelve followers, He laid out the significance of the tribulation... *the significance of the sign*. As they stood surveying the lights of the city, the ramification of the destruction of Jerusalem began to rush over the twelve.

The end of their world had been scheduled.

Jesus stated in the most emphatic, graphic, and biblical terms possible the significance of the destruction of the Old Covenant nation:

> "...the sun will be darkened, and the moon will not
> give its light, and the stars will fall from the sky..."
> (Matthew 24:29)

These were not strange words to the disciples. They knew the origin and interpretation of His words. From their youth they had heard these Old Testament symbols.

The writings of the prophets were filled with references to darkened suns, lightless moons, and falling stars. The prophets had used these terms to speak of the judgment of God. Now, Jesus was making the same statements. Therefore, the disciples knew the words of Jesus meant judgment was coming...the end of the apostate nation was at hand. They would witness the end of all that seemed most permanent and unshakable.

Everything giving the disciples' lives meaning or definition was about to be radically destroyed. The significance was certain. With the end of the city and its Temple, would come the end of the Old Covenant, and the end to the covenantal nation.

That damp spring night on the Mount of Olives the disciples of the Lord Jesus were facing the end of the age of Moses. They had committed their lives to follow a new prophet—one they were convinced to be the Messiah. As strange as it may have felt, they ultimately realized they were in reality following Moses by following Jesus. Both the Lord and Moses had agreed. Jesus had firmly insisted to the Jews:

> "If you believed Moses, you would believe Me; for he wrote of Me." (John 5:46)

Moses had predicted this Messianic moment. The great Old Covenant leader had prophesied that when the Messiah comes, every soul which does not heed that prophet will be utterly destroyed. With the destruction would come the end of the Old Covenant administration.

National Israel would never again hold the place of God's covenantal people. Her glory would be replaced by another nation...a nation producing the fruit of the Kingdom...the Church of Jesus Christ. Moses himself sang of this new nation. God would raise up a new people and provoke the children of Israel to jealousy:

> "I will make them jealous with those who are not a people;
>
> And I will provoke them to anger with a foolish nation..." (Deuteronomy 32:21)

The Apostle Paul referenced this song of Moses when he wrote to the Church at Rome. Speaking of the Jewish refusal to receive Jesus as Messiah, and the subsequent taking of the Gospel of the Kingdom to the Gentiles, Paul declared:

> "I say then, they did not stumble as to fall, did they? May it never be! But by their transgression salvation has come to the Gentiles, to make them jealous." (Romans 11:11)

Paul continued:

> "Behold then the kindness and severity of God; to
> those who fell, severity, but to you, God's kindness,
> if you continue in His kindness; otherwise you also
> will be cut off. And they also, if they do not contin-
> ue in their unbelief, will be grafted in; for God is
> able to graft them in again." (Romans 11:22-23)

Then Paul made his strongest statement concerning God's
dealing with the Jewish people during the saving rule of
King Jesus:

> "For I do not want you, brethren, to be uninformed
> of this mystery, lest you be wise in your own estima-
> tion, that a partial hardening has happened to Israel
> until the fullness of the Gentiles has come in; and
> thus all Israel will be saved..." (Romans 11:25-26)

The Mosaic administration with its sacrificial system legally ended at the cross of Jesus. The end of the Old Covenant
was a dramatic event. As Jesus hung on the cross, darkness
covered the whole land beginning at high noon. Around
three in the afternoon Jesus cried out:

> "It is finished!" (John 19:30)

When Jesus:

> "...cried out with a loud voice, and yielded His spirit.
> And behold, the veil of the temple was torn in two
> from the top to the bottom, and the earth shook;
> and the rocks were split, and tombs were opened;
> and many bodies of the saints who had fallen asleep
> were raised; and coming out of the tombs after His
> resurrection they entered the holy city and appeared
> to many. Now the centurion, and those who were

with him keeping guard over Jesus, when they saw
the things that were happening, became very frightened and said, 'Truly this was the Son of God!'"
(Matthew 27:50-54)

With the death of God's lamb the old sacrificial system was
completed. As the veil was torn in two, God left the Temple.
No longer would salvation be based upon the Law. The Old
Covenant was fulfilled!

The New Covenant began with the Lord's triumphant resurrection and ascension to the throne of David in heaven.
Yet, it would be forty years before the sign of this transition
would appear on the earth. The destruction of Jerusalem in
A.D. 70 would be the sign on the earth that the Old Covenant
age was ended, and the New Covenant had been fully inaugurated. On the basis of the New Covenant, Jesus would then
be administrating the Kingdom of Heaven as Messiah...King
of Kings and Lord of Lords.

But, there was another clause in Jesus' statement:

"...and the powers of the heavens will be shaken."
(Matthew 24:29)

Before the victory of Jesus at the cross, the entire world
was under the control of the kingdom of darkness. The
Kingdom of Heaven operated with Satan as the "ruler of the
world." Satan was able to blind nations and to keep them
under his power.

These were very familiar concepts to Jesus' disciples. The
Old Testament had clearly presented demonic powers behind
earthly thrones and civil governments. Daniel had spoken of
a demonic prince over Persia. The disciples were present when
Jesus addressed the religious leadership of Israel as children of
their father, the devil. The Apostle John would prophetically

see a demonized Rome as the tool of Satan's attack upon the infant Church.

In reality, God the Father was King over all Kingdoms. However, with the fall of man, the nations were under the influence of demonic powers, led by Satan. The disciples never saw this conflict as dualism, with a good god warring against an evil god. Rather, their revelation was one of a sovereign God who is ruler over all, being opposed by Satan, a created being who with a host of demonic beings functioned as outlaws until the time of the cross when they would be defeated by God's King—the Messiah.

With the coming of Messiah's Kingdom, the powers of the heavens—Satan and his angelic hierarchy—were to be shaken, chained and rendered powerless.

Long before the Olivet Discourse Jesus had promised the judgment of Satan. As the disciples returned from a preaching mission and reported demons were subject to them, Jesus reminded them of His authority and theirs:

> "I was watching Satan fall from heaven like lightning." (Luke 10:18)

Jesus was prophetically seeing Satan's kingdom destroyed. That destruction was the heavenly purpose for which He had come to earth. It would require His death on the cross to accomplish that purpose. As He revealed to His disciples the necessity of His death, He declared:

> "...For this purpose I came to this hour ... now the ruler of this world shall be cast out." (John 12:27-31)

Later the Apostle John would put it succinctly:

> "The Son of God appeared for this purpose, that He might destroy the works of the devil." (1 John 3:8)

The Apostle Paul defined the accomplishment of the Lord's purpose at the cross and resurrection when he declared:

> "When He had disarmed the rulers and authorities,
> He made a public display of them, having triumphed
> over them through Him." (Colossians 2:15)

The powers of heaven would be shaken by the Lord's death, resurrection, and ascension—Satan would be cast out of heaven! His authority would no longer be recognized. His ability to accuse the faithful would no longer be tolerated. His access to heaven would no longer be allowed.

In the Olivet Discourse, Jesus reminded His disciples of these earlier statements and clearly instructed them that they would experience this victory over the forces of Satan during their lives. As the Messianic Kingdom was established, the power of Satan's dominion over the earth would be destroyed.

It was by His death that Jesus:

> "...might render powerless him who had the power
> of death, that is, the devil; and might deliver those
> who through fear of death were subject to slavery all
> their lives." (Hebrews 2:14-15)

The Lord Jesus knew His victory over the kingdom of darkness would not be accomplished solely by His death and resurrection. Legally, He would defeat Satan at the cross. Satan would be judged—his legal power over the world would be destroyed—sin and death would be made powerless. Through Jesus' death and resurrection Satan would be cast out of heaven. However, he would be cast down to Earth to make war on the Saints—the disciples' generation of Saints. They would live through the transitional generation as the Old Covenant Jewish Kingdom was passing away and the New Testament Messianic Kingdom was being established.

The prophets were emphatic. Following Jesus' legal defeat of Satan on the cross, the Saints— the disciples' generation of Saints—would overcome Satan on earth:

"I kept looking, and that horn [demonized Nero] was waging war with the saints and overpowering them until the Ancient of Days came, and judgment was passed in favor of the saints of the Highest One, and the time arrived when the saints took possession of the kingdom." (Daniel 7:21-22)

Daniel saw the relentless persecution of the Church by Rome. Yet, he saw the victory of the early Church. The Saints would overcome Satan with their testimony and the power of the blood of Jesus. When the Lord ascended into heaven and received His Kingdom, He poured out the Holy Spirit upon the Church which enabled them to triumph! Satan had been judged!

Some years later, the power of the resurrected Christ and His Kingdom would be revealed to John. The Apostle would be ushered up into heaven to see the Messianic Kingdom inaugurated as Jesus ascended up to His Father in heaven. John would not see the Second Coming of Jesus, but the victory of the Lord's cross and resurrection:

"...for the accuser of our brethren has been thrown down, who accuses them before God day and night." (Revelation 12:10)

The Apostolic Revelator would look back at the cross and see its awesome accomplishment: the installation of Jesus as King of Kings and the casting down of the accuser!

Those disciples who stood with Jesus on the Mount of Olives that stormy spring evening would live to see the transition. Rather than the kingdom of Satan having dominion over the earth, Jesus' death, resurrection and ascension would establish His Messianic Kingdom. Then, as King of Kings, the Lord Jesus would bring His saving rule upon the earth. Those who had been made subject to death by the dominion of Satan would be free to receive the salvation of God. The power of Messiah's Kingdom would render Satan powerless over God's creation. With the outpouring of the Holy Spirit and the preaching of the Gospel of the Kingdom, *the powers of the heavens would be shaken.*

As certainly as the destruction of Jerusalem would indicate the end of the age of Moses and the beginning of the New Covenant, it would also be the sign on the earth of the casting down of the power of the devil. The sign would be for all to see. Its significance would change the world.

Yet, there was more. The destruction of the city in A.D. 70 would be the sign of the Son of Man reigning in heaven as King of Kings and Lord of Lords.

"Then shall appear the sign of the Son of Man in heaven..." (Matthew 24:30 KJV)

Jesus was in no way speaking of His Second Coming. To avoid any misconception, Jesus emphatically demanded that though the sign of His Kingdom would be on earth, He, the Son of Man, would be reigning in heaven.

Throughout His earthly ministry, the term Son of Man was a major emphasis for Jesus. He was constantly reinterpreting the Christology of His disciples. He, the Messiah, was to be understood as the Son of Man.

When they attributed to Him the title of Messiah, which brought with it the false Messianic hopes of the teachings of the apostate Jewish leaders of His day, Jesus adjusted them. Accepting their accolades as the Son of David, He would demand to be seen as the Son of Man.

Yes, He was the Messiah, but not the kind of Messiah they had expected. He had not come to establish an earthly, political, Jewish Kingdom—not then, not ever! He was to be understood as a Son of Man kind of Messiah, the Son of Man whose heavenly Kingdom had been prophesied by the Prophets.

When Jesus spoke of the Son of Man, He was referring to His heavenly reign. The disciples were thrilled, filled with excitement! Each word Jesus used was charged with Old Testament prophetic Messianic expectation. They recognized every phrase He used as a part of the heritage of their Old Testament faith. It was alive to them! Its significance was overwhelming. Before their very eyes the prophecies were being fulfilled.

The disciples emphatically believed the first coming of Jesus was not complete until Jesus returned to His Father and received His Kingdom. The great Old Testament prophets of Israel agreed. They had predicted this Son of Man Messiah reigning from the throne in heaven. The Prophet Daniel insisted:

"I kept looking in the night visions,
And behold, with the clouds of heaven
One like a Son of Man was coming,
And He came up to the Ancient of Days
And was presented before Him." (Daniel 7:13)

Daniel clearly saw the Son of Man coming up into heaven to receive His Kingdom. His rule would be from above. His throne would be in heaven. Daniel's vision was absolutely clear:

"He came up…
And to Him was given dominion,
Glory and a kingdom,

That all the peoples, nations, and men of
every language
Might serve Him.
His dominion is an everlasting dominion
Which will not pass away;
And His kingdom is one
Which will not be destroyed." (Dan 7:13-14)

Daniel was not speaking of the Second Coming! According to Daniel, Messiah's Kingdom, the Kingdom of the Son of Man would begin with His ascension, not His Second Coming. He would come up to the Ancient of Days and receive a Kingdom which would never pass away. There was no word of coming down to earth and establishing an earthly, political, Jewish Kingdom. Messiah's Kingdom would be a Kingdom over all peoples, nations and languages. It would be a heavenly Kingdom with earthly authority.

Every Prophet of the Old Testament had seen the same Kingdom. Even King David had seen the heavenly Kingdom of the Son of God:

"But as for Me I have installed My King Upon Zion,
My holy mountain." (Psalm 2:7)

This was David's great enthronement Psalm which would be fulfilled in the resurrection and ascension of the Lord Jesus. The early Church placed great importance upon this Psalm of David. Based upon David's prophetic declaration, the disciples fully believed Zion, the location of Jesus' throne, was in heaven. They understood and taught this heavenly Mount Zion to be the capitol city of Messiah's Kingdom.

This was extremely important to the disciples. As they went about the task of preaching the Gospel of the Kingdom and building the Church, they did so with a pure belief in the heavenly reign of King Jesus. The Kingdom in which they served was a heavenly Kingdom. They saw themselves as citizens of the heavenly Jerusalem—the city of the living God:

> "You have come to Mount Zion and to the city of
> the living God, the heavenly Jerusalem…"
> (Hebrews 12:22)

There was no question in the hearts of the disciples. Jesus was reigning with absolute power. All authority had been given to their King! He was Lord over all. This was a critical understanding to the Church.

The Apostle Paul indicated the power and authority which the early Church believed Jesus enjoyed in this heavenly city:

> "…and what is the surpassing greatness of His power
> toward us who believe. These are in accordance with
> the working of the strength of His might which He
> brought about in Christ, when He raised Him from
> the dead, and seated Him at His right hand in the
> heavenly places, far above all rule and authority and
> power and dominion, and every name that is named,
> not only in this age, but also in the one to come.
> And He put all things in subjection under His feet,
> and gave Him as head over all things to the Church,
> which is His body, the fullness of Him who fills all
> in all." (Ephesians 1:19-23)

This was the foundational truth to the early Church. Jesus was Lord—King! The disciples never believed Jesus was waiting for His Kingdom. The idea of the Lord's reign being postponed to some future millennium would have been ridiculous to the disciples and the early Church. They believed they were living in His Kingdom. They taught His Kingdom was a heavenly Kingdom—not of this world, not then, not ever!

A few weeks following Jesus' Olivet Discourse, the Apostle Peter stood on the Day of Pentecost and preached to the crowd of Jews who had gathered from "every nation under heaven." In his sermon the Apostle used David's prophetic vision of the resurrected Son of God as proof Jesus had ascended to the Father and received His Kingdom. The Lord's Kingdom had been inaugurated at His resurrection and ascension into heaven:

> "Because David was a prophet, and knew that God
> had sworn to him with an oath to seat one of his
> descendants upon his throne, David looked ahead
> and spoke of the resurrection of Christ..."
> (Acts 2:30-31)

The Apostle was emphatic!

Peter further demanded that the outpouring of the Holy Spirit on the day of Pentecost was the Father's affirmation that Jesus was reigning as King of Kings and Lord of Lords:

> "This Jesus God raised up again, to which we are all
> witnesses.
> "Therefore having been exalted to the right hand of
> God, and having received from the Father the
> promise of the Holy Spirit, He has poured forth this
> which you both see and hear..."
> 'Therefore let all the house of Israel know for certain
> that God has made Him both Lord and Christ...'"
> (Acts 2:32, 33, 36)

He was not waiting to be Lord—Jesus was Lord! He was not waiting to be the Christ, the Messiah, the King—Jesus was the Christ! The outpouring of the Holy Spirit on the day of Pentecost was the proof of his Kingship.

Later in his apostolic ministry, the Apostle Peter boldly proclaimed Jesus was:

"*At the right hand of God [the place of all authority and power]*, having gone into heaven, *after* angels and authorities and powers had been subjected to Him."
(1 Pet. 3:22)

The Apostle Peter was not the only Apostle to make this strong point. The Apostle Paul also interpreted David's second Psalm as proof of God's promise of a Messianic Kingdom being fulfilled by the Lord's present reign in heaven:

"God has fulfilled this promise to our children in that He raised up Jesus, as it is also written in the second Psalm..." (Acts 13:33)

Once again, the Apostle Paul reached back to King David's great enthronement Psalm. It was this Psalm which prophetically envisioned God's anointed King–His Christ, the Messiah, David's greater Son–sitting on David's throne in heaven and reigning as King of Kings and Lord of Lords.

"But as for Me, I have installed [enthroned] My King
Upon Zion, My Holy Mountain.
'I will surely tell of the decree of the Lord:
He said to Me, 'Thou art My Son,
Today I have begotten Thee'..." (Psalm 2:6-7)

The Apostle Paul had to have wrestled with this famous Psalm of David. When did this happen? When was God's King installed? When was His Son begotten? The Apostle's answer to these critical questions established the doctrine of the Church and the message they would preach:

"And we preach to you the good news of the promise made to the fathers, that God has fulfilled this promise to our children in that He raised up Jesus, as it is also written in the second Psalm, 'Thou art My Son; today I have begotten Thee.' And as for the fact that He raised Him up from the dead, no more to return to decay, He has spoken in this way: 'I will give you the holy and sure blessings of David.'" (Acts 13:32-34)

The Apostle Paul declared the gospel was the "good news" that God had fulfilled His promises to the fathers of Israel, specifically His promise to David concerning the installation of David's son to sit on David's throne, in the resurrection of Jesus. Then Paul took the same Psalm the Apostle Peter had used at Pentecost and declared:

"Therefore He also says in another Psalm, 'Thou wilt not allow thy Holy One to undergo decay.' For David, after he had served the purpose of God in his own generation, fell asleep, and was laid among his fathers, and underwent decay; but He whom God raised did not undergo decay." (Acts 13:35-37)

The Apostle Paul then rebuked the Jews at Antioch with a powerful reminder of the work which God had completed in His Son, the Lord Jesus:

"Therefore let it be known to you, brethren, that through Him forgiveness of sins is proclaimed to you, and through Him everyone who believes is freed from all things, from which you could not be freed through the Law of Moses. Take heed therefore, so that the thing spoken of in the Prophets may not come upon you: 'Behold, you scoffers, and marvel, and perish; for I am accomplishing a work in your days, a work which you will never believe, though someone should describe it to you.'" (Acts 13:38-41)

The Apostle Peter and the Apostle Paul were in agreement. Jesus had conquered death, defeated Satan, and established the New Covenant Kingdom in His own blood. No power in heaven or on Earth remained to be conquered. His authority was absolute. He had been raised from the dead, installed on the throne of God, and was reigning as King of Kings and Lord of Lords. The promise God had made to David concerning His son sitting on his throne had been fulfilled by the resurrection, ascension and enthronement of Jesus of Nazareth. Because of His resurrection, Jesus would sit on the throne of the Kingdom of Heaven and reign as God. In the Old Covenant, David's throne on earth had represented God's throne in heaven. David, as God's anointed king, ruled Israel and the nations from Mount Zion in Jerusalem. Under the New Covenant administrated by Jesus of Nazareth the Son of David, the Son of God would sit on God's throne in heaven, or as David had prophesied:

> "The Lord says to my Lord:
> 'Sit at My right hand,
> Until I make Thine enemies a footstool for Thy feet.'
> The Lord will stretch forth Thy strong scepter from
> Zion, saying,
> 'Rule in the midst of Thine enemies.'"
> (Psalm 110:1-3)

God's throne in heaven would become David's throne. And David's Lord, His greater Son, the Son of God, would rule the nations of the earth from God's throne in heaven. David prophetically saw Zion as the heavenly mountain and Messiah's scepter—representing His authority and rule—that would stretch forth from the heavenly Jerusalem.

This was the heavenly sign which Jesus had promised to His disciples that damp night on the Mount of Olives:

> "Then shall appear the sign of the Son of Man
> in heaven..." (Matthew 24:30 KJV)

The sign on earth, the destruction of Jerusalem by the armies of Rome, would declare to the world: Jesus is King! The destruction of earthly Jerusalem would be the physical sign that the Son of God was reigning in His Messianic Kingdom—ruling over the nations from the city of God—the heavenly Jerusalem—Mount Zion!

The destruction of Jerusalem would also signify that the judgment of the nations had begun.

The way in which the Lord dealt with Israel during the transitional generation would serve as the prophetic model of how kings and kingdoms would be judged throughout the ages of Messiah's heavenly Kingdom. The destruction of Jerusalem and the nation of Israel in A.D. 70 would also serve as a warning to Gentile governments and nations: be converted or be destroyed—"kiss the Son or perish!"

On the Mount of Olives, Jesus stipulated the disciples must preach the Gospel of the Kingdom to the Israelites scattered throughout the Roman Empire. Before God's judgment would come upon the apostate nation, the Lord would entreat them with a covenant of peace, an offer of mercy and grace, an opportunity to obey the Gospel of the Kingdom and receive His salvation:

> "This Gospel of the Kingdom shall be preached in
> the whole world for a witness to all the nations, and
> then shall the end come." (Matthew 24:14)

Those Israelites who responded positively to the Gospel were gathered as the remnant and formed into the body of Christ. However, the nation as a whole refused the Lord's offer of salvation, His mercy and grace, and was destroyed in A.D. 70.

The pattern of judgment was established.

Just as Christ judged Jerusalem and the nation of Israel on the basis of their response to the Gospel of the Kingdom, so throughout His reign He would judge the nations of the earth.

As the disciples stood viewing Jerusalem from the Mount of Olives, Jesus made it perfectly clear to His disciples: any and every nation which refused the Lord's rule would face the same heavenly judgment as Jerusalem.

"...then shall all the tribes of the earth mourn..." (Matthew 24:30)

The Lord had predicted the inevitable. When the nations of the earth view the Lord's judgment of apostate Israel–the destruction of Jerusalem, the decimation of the Temple, the carnage of the people, the end of the society of Moses–they would mourn. Their mourning would be understandable. For just as the lord had judged the nation of Israel, He would also judge them.

Not only would the nations mourn, they would also see:

"...the Son of Man coming on the clouds of the sky with power and great glory." (Matthew 24: 30)

When Jesus spoke of coming on the clouds, He was using technical language which He did not invent. He was using Old Testament language to speak of His own government and power to judge nations. King David described the Kingdom of God of the Old Testament. He saw the Father of the Lord Jesus parting the heavens and coming in His cloud chariot to judge His enemies and to deliver His servant David.

"He bowed the heavens also, and came down
With thick darkness under His feet.
And He rode upon a cherub and flew;
And He sped upon the wings of the wind.
He made darkness His hiding place, His canopy
around Him,
Darkness of water, thick clouds of the skies."
(Psalm 18:9-11)

The great Old Testament Prophet Ezekiel was in agreement with David's understanding regarding clouds. To Ezekiel, the day of the Lord was a day of great power. As he prophetically described the judgment day of the Lord, he saw a day of clouds.

"...the day of the Lord is near;
It will be a day of clouds,
A time of doom for the nations." (Ezekiel 30:3)

Ezekiel was not speaking of the Second Coming of Christ or the end of the world. Rather, he was prophesying the judgment of God upon Egypt which would take place in Ezekiel's day.

On the Mount of Olives the Lord Jesus used the same Old Testament language to describe to His disciples the workings of His day—Messiah's day. From the heavenly throne of His father David, Jesus would be seen judging the nations—coming on the clouds of the sky with power and great glory. The Lord would be in heaven ruling, but His judgments would be manifest on Earth. As a result of His judgment of Israel in A.D. 70, the nations would understand the time had come in the history of the world for them to acknowledge Jesus as Lord and receive His government.

Legally, the judgment of the nations would begin at the cross. As "the hour" of His death drew near, He demanded:

"Now is the judgment of this world..."
(John 12:31 KJV)

The decisive judgment of the world took place at the crucifixion. However, practically and progressively, His judgment (discipline) of the nations would continue throughout His administration of the Kingdom of Heaven. The final judgment of the nations would take place at the consummation of His Kingdom with His Second Coming.

As He talked with His disciples on the Mount of Olives, Jesus had the Old Testament prophets clearly in view. He declared to His disciples:

"...then all the tribes of the earth will mourn, and
they will see the Son of Man coming on the clouds
of the sky with power and great glory."
(Matthew 24:30)

Jesus was not describing His Second Coming at the end of the world. Instead He was declaring to His disciples that the destruction of Jerusalem, the harlot city, and Herod's Temple in A.D. 70 would be the sign to the Gentiles that the judgment of the nations had begun. Beginning with the ancient city and the House of God, His judgments would continue until all governments and nations have been brought under the discipline of God's anointed King.

The significance of the sign of the Kingdom, the destruction of Jerusalem and the Temple, was obvious to these apostles and the early Church following Jesus' resurrection and triumphant ascension. They fully believed Jesus was in heaven reigning as King! The Old Covenant of Moses had legally ended. The New Covenant had been established and the promised Holy Spirit poured out. Satan had been defeated and the Messianic Kingdom fully inaugurated.

As King of Kings and Lord of Lords, Jesus would send His Apostles into all the world to offer His salvation to the nations. By the power of the Holy Spirit, they would preach the Gospel of the Kingdom to the peoples of the earth. The nations would either obey His Gospel, be converted and receive the blessings of salvation, or they would be destroyed by the judgments of His Kingdom.

As God's anointed King, He would ride the clouds with His heavenly army, the Church, judging and making war on the kingdom of darkness, setting the nations free and establishing justice in the earth.

The judgment of the nations has begun!

8

THE SUCCESS OF THE SIGN

The intensity was overpowering! As evening had captured the Mount of Olives late that Tuesday night, so Jesus had captivated the disciples with the radical significance His heavenly reign would have on the nation of Israel. They fixated on every word He spoke. Slowly, the Lord searched their faces. Every word was directed to them. Just as the disciples were to play major roles in the success of the First Apostolic Mission—the Jewish Mission preceding the destruction of Jerusalem—they and those who would come after them would also be dominant participants in the successful events of the Second Apostolic Mission—the Gentile Mission which would follow the destruction of Jerusalem—the sign of the Kingdom.

Jesus was completely confident in the success of His Kingdom. He would insure its success. Immediately after the sign occurred, King Jesus was to:

"...send forth His angels with a great trumpet and they will gather together His elect from the four

winds, from one end of the sky to the other."
(Matthew 24:31)

This would be the Gentile Mission and it would succeed. No longer would God be covenantally committed to physical Israel. Through the victorious reign of His Son, the King of Heaven, righteousness would fill the whole earth, every nation. Christ's Apostles would be His instruments as He launched the Second Apostolic Mission. During this mission the Gospel of the Kingdom would be trumpeted to all the nations of the world, " from the four winds, from one end of the sky to the other." Once again the Son of Man would send forth His messengers. But, following the destruction of Jerusalem, no longer to the Jews first.

This was a critical moment during the Olivet Discourse. Had it not been for the parable Jesus used with His disciples earlier that day, they might have thought Jesus was speaking of the final judgment at the end of the world. But, during His parable of the wedding feast, the Lord presented the chronology of Kingdom events which He would unfold in the Olivet Discourse: A king gave a wedding feast for his son. He sent out messengers to gather the invited guests, the Jews, yet, they would not come. Ultimately, those invited to the feast kill the king's messengers. The king is outraged and burns their city. Thus Jesus parabolically described the First Apostolic Mission—the Jewish Mission—which officially ended with the burning of the city—the destruction of Jerusalem by the Romans in A.D. 70. In the Olivet Discourse Jesus referred to this first mission and its tragic ending with the solemn words:

"And this Gospel of the Kingdom shall be preached
in the whole world for a witness to all the nations,
and then the end shall come." (Matthew. 24:14)

Peter and his brothers would preach the Gospel to the Jews scattered throughout the inhabited earth. They would gather the believing remnant of Israel from throughout the Roman Empire who together with the believing Gentiles—the firstfruits of the nations—would form the New Covenant Israel. Once the Jewish Mission had been completed with the successful formation of the New Covenant people of God, the Jewish age would come to an end! Jerusalem would be destroyed by fire—the sign that the Kingdom of Messiah had been established.

But there was more. In Jesus' prophetic parable, following the prophesied end of Jerusalem—the city which would not respond to the invitation of the king—the king sent his servants into the main highways to gather those who would fill the banquet hall. This was the Second Apostolic Mission, the Gentile Mission. This was the exact chronology of Kingdom events which Jesus followed in the Olivet Discourse.

> "And He will send forth His angels with a great trumpet and they will gather together His elect from the four winds, from one end of the sky to the other." (Matthew. 24:31)

Contrary to popular belief, Jesus was not describing the sending forth of magnificent, supernatural, winged, angelic beings to gather His Saints at the end of the world! Nor was He depicting the re-gathering and future conversion of physical Israel after the Second Coming as some presuppose! Instead, He was describing the Second Apostolic Mission, the mission to the Gentiles, which would continue until all the nations of the earth have been successfully discipled.

Jesus spoke of the times of the Gentiles:

> "Woe to those who are with child and to those who nurse babes in those days; for there will be great distress upon the land, and wrath to this people, and they will fall by the edge of the sword, and will be

led captive into all the nations; and Jerusalem will be trampled under foot by the Gentiles until the times of the Gentiles be fulfilled." (Luke 21:23-24)

There on the Mount of Olives overlooking the ancient city and its Temple, as the Lord prophesied the destruction of Jerusalem and its sanctuary, His words flooded the disciples with mixed emotions. Their beloved city would be destroyed and even trampled under foot, yet the Gentile Mission would be fulfilled. However, as the mission to the nations was being fulfilled, there remained a promise, a hope for Israel. The Lord Jesus had used the time word "until." Jerusalem would be trampled until the Gentile Mission was successfully completed—until the nations were filled with the Glory of God.

This was the conviction of the disciples.

The Apostle Paul would also voice the same time word in his treatise to the Saints at Rome. He would declare:

"...a partial hardening has happened to Israel until the fullness of the Gentiles has come in..."
(Romans 11:25)

That partial hardness would result in the destruction of Jerusalem, the Temple, and the cutting off of the nation. However, the hearts of the Jewish people would not always be hardened. The time would come when the fullness of the Gentiles—the success of the Gentile Mission—would come into the Kingdom and as a direct result the hardness would be removed. According to the Apostle Paul, the hearts of the Jewish people would some day be provoked to jealousy by seeing the blessings of the Messianic Kingdom come upon the Gentiles because of their obedience of the Gospel. At that time the hardness would be removed, the Jewish people would be provoked to jealousy, repent from their sins, receive Jesus as their Lord, fully obey the Gospel and be grafted back into the people of God.

Standing in the Temple courts only a few hours before hearing His Olivet discourse, the disciples heard Jesus make that very declaration. Prophesying the destruction of Jerusalem and the Temple, He declared to the apostate leadership of Israel:

> "...you shall not see Me until you say, 'Blessed is He who comes in the name of the Lord!'"
> (Matthew 23:39)

Amazingly, Jesus declared they would not see Him again until they repented of their unbelief and rebellion, and believed in the Lord and His messengers. According to Jesus, their future beholding of Him would not take place until they first believed in Him and confessed Him as the Christ. This is the exact opposite of what some have taught. In spite of what some believe, the future conversion of Israel will not be the result of their physically seeing Him at His return. Instead, their beholding Him in the Second Coming will be the result of their first believing and confessing Him as the one sent in the name of the Father. The Lord's Second Coming will be, at least in part, the result of Israel's yet future turning from her rebellion and hardness of heart, and fully obeying the Gospel.

Jesus made absolutely no mention of His Second Coming in the Olivet Discourse. Rather, Jesus emphatically declared a critically important eschatological fact! The destruction of Jerusalem would be the sign on Earth, the great time indicator, and the single historical demonstration that the Jewish Mission and God's salvific dealings with the Jewish nation had ended and the Gentile Mission or "the times of the Gentiles" had officially begun.

Only a few hours before, standing in the court of the Gentiles in the Temple, Jesus had prophesied that the Kingdom of the Messiah would be taken from the unbelieving nation and be given to the New Covenant Nation which would be made up of the believing remnant of Israel and the firstfruits of the Gentiles. Ultimately, this New Nation, the True Israel, His Church, would be the instrument of His Kingdom purpose to disciple the Gentile nations and fill the earth with the glory of God. In His Olivet Discourse, He declared prophetically that Jerusalem would be trodden under foot until the Gentile Mission had succeeded and the fullness of the Gentiles had been brought into the Kingdom.

The Apostle Paul had anticipated these events as His own ministry drew to a close. While he was under house arrest, the leaders of the Jewish community in Rome came together to hear Paul speak about the Kingdom of God. While some were persuaded, others refused to believe the Gospel. Because of their hard heartedness and opposition, Paul prophesied to them:

> "The Holy Spirit rightly spoke through Isaiah the prophet to your fathers, saying, 'Go to this people and say, 'You will keep on hearing, but will not understand; and you will keep on seeing, but will not perceive; for the heart of this people has become dull, and with their ears they scarcely hear, and they have closed their eyes; lest they should see with their eyes, and hear with their ears, and understand with their heart and return, and I should heal them.' Let it be known to you therefore, that this salvation of God has been sent to the Gentiles; they will also listen." (Acts 28:25-28)

The Apostle Paul dealt with this specific issue in his letter to the Romans. He boldly proclaimed:

> "...that a partial hardening has happened to Israel until the fullness of the Gentiles has come in."
> (Romans 11:25)

While Jesus' phrase, "the times of the Gentiles" and Paul's phrase, "the fullness of the Gentiles" are not synonymous, they are most certainly related. Both concern the Second Apostolic Mission—the mission to the Gentiles. This Gentile period will continue until all the nations have been fully disciplined or until the fullness of the Gentiles has been brought into Messiah's Kingdom.

In these significant words, "the fullness of the Gentiles," Paul was prophetically anticipating the success of the Lord's Gentile Mission; envisioning whole nations being discipled and brought into the Kingdom, resulting in the establishment of Christian nations and cultures. According to the Apostle Paul, it is the ultimate success of this Second Apostolic Mission, the Gentile Mission and not the Second Coming, which will bring about the future repentance and conversion of natural Israel:

> "...and thus all Israel will be saved; just as it is written, 'The Deliverer will come from Zion, He will remove ungodliness from Jacob.'" (Romans. 11:26)

The Apostle was not seeing the Second Coming. He was in agreement with words of the Lord Jesus:

> "For I say to you, from now on you shall not see Me until you say, 'Blessed is He who comes in the name of the Lord!'" (Matthew. 23:39)

Jesus had avowed that Israel would not see Him again until they had repented of their unbelief and were converted, confessing Jesus of Nazareth as Lord and Christ.

Paul is markedly transparent in his agreement with Jesus! He reveals that the key to the future conversion and restoration of the nation of Israel is not the removal of the Church in some imagined secret rapture, or the bodily appearance of

Christ in His Second Coming. Instead, it is the simple principle of provocation!

In the larger context of his letter to the Romans, Paul, as did Jesus before him, quotes from the Song of Moses:

> "But I say, surely Israel did not know, did they? At the first Moses says, 'I will make you jealous by that which is not a nation, by a nation without understanding will I anger you.' And Isaiah is very bold and says, 'I was found by those who sought Me not, I became manifest to those who did not ask for Me.' But as for Israel He says, 'All the day long I have stretched out My hands to a disobedient and obstinate people.'" (Romans. 10:19-21)

Paul succinctly articulated the principle of provocation:

> "I say then, they did not stumble so as to fall, did they? May it never be! But by their transgression salvation has come to the Gentiles, to make them jealous. Now if their transgression be riches for the world and their failure be riches for the Gentiles, how much more will their fulfillment be!"
> (Romans. 11:11-13)

When "the fullness of the Gentiles" has been brought in, the hardness will be removed from the nation. Beholding the full blessings of the Messianic Kingdom coming upon the believing and obedient Gentile nations will cause the unbelieving and disobedient nation of Israel to be provoked to jealousy and be converted. Those Israelites who are converted will be grafted back into the Lord's olive tree.

According to the Apostle Paul, the future salvation of unbelieving Israel will not be the result of the Second Coming. It will be the result of the Church's success in its mission to disciple the nations. It will be the result of the principle of provocation!

The fullness of the Gentiles and the fullness of the Jews together will make up the "fullness of Christ" which Paul prophesied to the Ephesian Church:

> "...until we all attain to the unity of the faith, and of the knowledge of the Son of God, to a mature man, to the measure of the stature which belongs to the fullness of Christ." (Ephesians 4:13-15)

In order to fully comprehend the Olivet Discourse, the present reign of Jesus Christ, and the Church's immediate mission to the nations as it relates to the unfolding of God's Kingdom purpose, it is imperative to understand the chronological order of these two distinctive apostolic missions—the Jewish Mission and the Gentile Mission, separated from each other by the burning of Jerusalem by the Romans in A.D. 70.

It is also critically important to understand that after His resurrection Jesus actually gave the disciples two apostolic commissions, the Judean and the Galilean. In reverse order to their fulfillment, the Galilean commission, corresponding to the Gentile mission, was given first. The Judean, corresponding to the Jewish Mission, occurred immediately prior to Jesus' ascension. While they are similar in many respects, each is distinct and essential to the fulfillment of Christ's Kingdom purpose.

The first was given on a mountain in Galilee. In this Galilean commission, the so-called "great commission," Jesus prophetically anticipated the Gentile mission. After His resurrection, Jesus had instructed Mary Magdalene and the other Mary to tell His disciples to meet Him in Galilee. They obeyed:

> "...the eleven disciples proceeded to Galilee to the
> mountain which Jesus had designated."
> (Matthew 28:16)

This particular mountain and the Sea of Galilee which it over-
looked had come to prophetically signify to Jesus and His disciples the nations of the earth. Its memories were glorious. On
that same mountain, Jesus had given His sermon proclaiming
for Israel and for the nations of the earth the laws of His
Messianic Kingdom.

There also, on two momentous occasions, He had miracu-
lously fed great crowds with a few small fish and some loaves
of bread. These were not random acts. Isaiah had prophesied:

> "And the LORD of hosts will prepare a lavish ban-
> quet for all peoples on this mountain; a banquet of
> aged wine, choice pieces with marrow, and refined,
> aged wine."

> "And it will be said in that day, 'Behold, this is our
> God for whom we have waited that He might save
> us. This is the LORD for whom we have waited; let
> us rejoice and be glad in His salvation.'"
> (Isaiah 25:6, 9)

These miracle feedings had been prophetic actions signifying
to Israel Jesus was the promised Messiah. He had indeed come
down from God out of heaven to prepare for Israel and all
nations a lavish banquet, a great banquet of salvation. Every
human need would be met! Satan would be defeated. Satanic
principalities and powers would be destroyed. Sin would be
removed. Sickness and disease would be healed. Demons
would be driven out of people's lives. Marriages, families,
economies and civil governments would be changed. Whole
nations and cultures would be transformed by His power and
glory. Later, these same disciples would realize the Lord Jesus

would not only be the host of this great heavenly banquet; He, Himself, would also be the meal. At the Lord's table, His body and blood would provide the food of salvation not only for Israel, but for the whole world, for all who believe.

Remembering these momentous events, the eleven were filled with wonderful excitement and anticipation. Suddenly Jesus appeared to them and triumphantly declared:

> "All authority has been given to Me in heaven and on earth..." (Matthew 28:18)

The Messianic Kingdom had not been postponed! It had been given to Jesus! His resurrection attested to this fact! All the authority and power of the Kingdom of God had been given to Him. He was after all the promised Son of David, the very Son of God, who would sit in resurrection glory upon the throne of His Kingdom in Heaven and rule the nations forever.

On the basis of His Kingdom authority, Jesus commissioned His Apostles:

> "Go therefore and make disciples of all the nations,
> baptizing them in the name of the Father and the
> Son and the Holy Spirit, teaching them to observe all
> that I commanded you; and lo, I am with you
> always, even to the end of the age."
> (Matthew 28:19-20)

Disciple the nations! Bring them under His government, His discipline, the righteous judgment of God's King. Not just some—but all! Not merely evangelizing every racial or ethnic group in the world, but bringing the moral and spiritual government of God to every political and geographic entity on Earth until all nations have learned Christ.

The Lord's gracious and merciful dealings with Israel during the period of the Jewish Mission would serve as the pattern of His dealings with the nations throughout the times of the Gentiles. Throughout His reign, Jesus of Nazareth, as King of Kings and Lord of Lords, would judge the Gentile nations on the basis of their response to the Gospel of the Kingdom. And the destruction of Jerusalem in A.D. 70 would serve as a warning to all nations throughout the entire period of the Gentile Mission. Just as Israel could not escape the judgment of God, neither would the Gentile nations.

As Jesus looked upon the Sea of Galilee, He thought of the nations of the earth—His God-given inheritance. He envisioned the "times of the Gentiles" which would follow the judgment of Israel. He envisioned the heavenly life of His Messianic Kingdom filling and transforming the people of all the nations of the earth, and prophetically commissioned the Second Apostolic Mission—the Gentile Mission to the nations.

But there was another commission, the Judean. According to Luke, this second commission occurred on the Mount of Olives just outside Jerusalem in the region of Judea at the time of the Lord's ascension. On this occasion Jesus commissioned Peter and his brothers to be His witnesses and to preach the Gospel of the Kingdom to the Jews scattered throughout the world:

> "...but you shall receive power when the Holy Spirit
> has come upon you; and you shall be My witnesses
> both in Jerusalem, and in all Judea and Samaria, and
> even to the remotest part of the earth." (Acts 1:8)

This was the first Apostolic Mission—the Jewish Mission. The Apostles, empowered by the Spirit of God, would be sent to gather the remnant of Israel and the firstfruits of the Gentiles from throughout the Roman Empire. Founded upon the long promised redemption in Christ and the New Covenant in His blood, together, they would form the New Covenant Israel. The formation of this new nation would signal the fulfillment of the Old Covenant and the promises God had made to the fathers of Israel. Then the Messianic Kingdom would be taken from the unbelieving nation and be given to the new. This new Israel would be the instrument of Messiah's Kingdom to disciple the nations bringing them under His moral and spiritual government. This Jewish Mission would officially end with the burning of Jerusalem and the Temple.

After this commission, Jesus was lifted up in a cloud of glory and ascended into heaven. Just ten days later, on the Day of Pentecost, the promised Holy Spirit was poured out upon the waiting Apostles and the rest of the Church as the witness of the Father that Jesus had been glorified and enthroned as God's anointed King. Beginning in Jerusalem the Apostles went into Jewish synagogues throughout the Roman Empire and gave their witness in fulfillment of the Lord's prophetic promise given in the Olivet Discourse:

"And this Gospel of the Kingdom shall be preached
in the whole world for a witness to all the nations,
and then the end shall come." (Matthew 24:14)

In spite of great opposition and much difficulty, the Jewish Mission ultimately succeeded. The early Church was predominately Jewish. The book of Acts, the Epistles, and the book of Revelation all record the successful gathering of the believing remnant of Israel and the firstfruits of the Gentiles.

Ironically Paul, recognized by the early Church as the Apostle to the Gentiles, described himself as one born out of the proper time (I Corinthians 15:8). Commissioned to bring the Gentile nations to obedience to Christ, he labored during the period of the Jewish Mission. The times of the Gentiles and the Gentile Mission would not begin until the end of the Jewish age and the successful completion of the Jewish Mission.

Throughout his ministry the Apostle Paul recognized and honored the season in which he worked. In doing so, upon his arrival in a Gentile city, he always went immediately to the Jewish synagogue. Though he was the Apostle to the Gentiles even his ministry was first to the Jews.

Contrary to what some teach today, Paul taught that the Old Testament promises concerning the gathering of the remnant of Israel were being fulfilled in his own day! According to the Apostle Paul, he himself along with the other Jewish believers in the early Church, constituted that prophesied remnant:

> "I say then, God has not rejected His people, has He? May it never be! For I too am an Israelite, a descendant of Abraham, of the tribe of Benjamin. God has not rejected His people whom He foreknew. Or do you not know what the Scripture says in the passage about Elijah, how he pleads with God against Israel? 'Lord, they have killed Thy prophets, they have torn down Thine altars, and I alone am left, and they are seeking my life.' But what is the divine response to him? 'I have kept for Myself seven thousand men who have not bowed the knee to Baal.' In the same way then, *there has also come to be at the present time a remnant according to God's gracious choice.*" (Romans 11:1-5)

Not only was this Jewish remnant being successfully gathered together in Paul's day, the Apostle declared this believing remnant had already obtained the promises of God concerning Messiah's Kingdom:

"What then? That which Israel is seeking for, it has not obtained, but *those who were chosen obtained it...*" (Romans 11:7)

Paul could not have been more clear. The chosen remnant of Israelites who made up the nucleus of the early Church had "obtained" the very things Israel had been diligently seeking! They had already received the fulfillment of the promises God made to their fathers concerning the Messianic Kingdom, the age of the Spirit and the salvation of God!

Many today radically disagree with Paul. They reject his apostolic claim of the early Church having obtained the things which Israel had been seeking. For them, the Messianic Kingdom has been postponed. The promises, which God made to the patriarchs of Israel, are being held in abeyance awaiting their fulfillment to a yet to be re-gathered Jewish remnant in a future, earthly, Jewish, millennial kingdom at the Second Coming.

But the Apostle Paul was adamant. He insisted the believing remnant of Israel of his own day had already successfully obtained the Kingdom!

But that was not all. Paul demanded not only the believing Jews, but the firstfruits of the Gentiles also had obtained the fulfillment of the promises which God had made to Abraham and his seed concerning Messiah's Kingdom. These Gentile believers were being gathered during the season of the Jewish Mission in prophetic anticipation of the Gentile Mission and its future success. The firstfruits ultimately promised the full harvest of the nations. Paul avowed:

"Therefore, be sure that it is *those who are of faith who are sons of Abraham*. And the Scripture, foreseeing that God would *justify the Gentiles by faith*, preached the gospel beforehand to Abraham, saying, '*All the nations* shall be blessed in you.'"

"Christ redeemed us from the curse of the Law...that in Christ Jesus *the blessing of Abraham might come to the Gentiles,* so that we might receive the promise of the Spirit through faith."

"Now *the promises were spoken to Abraham and to his seed.* He does not say, 'And to seeds,' as referring to many, but rather to one, 'And to your seed,' *that is, Christ.*"

"Why the Law then? It was added because of trans-gressions...*until the seed should come to whom the promise had been made.*"

"But the Scripture has shut up all men under sin, that the promise by faith in Jesus Christ might be given to those who believe."

"For you are all sons of God through faith in Christ Jesus. For all of you who were baptized into Christ have clothed yourselves with Christ...And *if you belong to Christ, then you are Abraham's offspring, heirs according to promise.*"
(Galatians 3:7-9, 13-14, 16, 19, 22, 26-29)

The promises belong to Abraham's seed, Jesus Christ. He died on the cross without a natural descendent or fleshly heir. Therefore the Abrahamic promises cannot belong to flesh, even Jewish flesh, but only to those born of the Spirit. Jesus Christ died and rose again to bring forth a new creation, a new species of being–neither Jew nor Gentile! He died and rose again so that both Jew and Gentile might be born of the Spirit of God, become the children of God by faith in Christ Jesus, receive the indwelling presence of the Holy Spirit, and become full heirs of all the promises God made to Abraham. The Apostle proclaimed, only those who have believed in

Jesus Christ, being baptized into His death and raised up into His life are truly Abraham's seed. Thus, no one, Jew or Gentile, inherits a single promise except through faith in Jesus Christ.

In spite of the Apostle's word to the contrary many stubbornly insist that the promises God made to Abraham belong exclusively to Jewish flesh. But Paul disagreed. Quoting Isaiah, he reminded the Galatians:

> "For it is written, 'Rejoice, *barren woman* who does
> not bear; break forth and shout, you who are not in
> labor; for more are the children of the desolate than
> of the one who has a husband.' And *you brethren*, like
> Isaac, *are children of promise*. But as at that time he
> who was born according to the flesh persecuted him
> who was born according to the Spirit, so it is now
> also. But what does the Scripture say? 'Cast out the
> bondwoman and her son, for the son of the bond-
> woman shall not be an heir with the son of the free
> woman.' So then, brethren, *we are not children of a
> bondwoman, but of the free woman.*" (Galatians 4:27-31)

Believers, not only Jewish but also Gentile, were the true "children of promise!" Born of God's Spirit, they were the children of the free woman, the Heavenly Jerusalem. They—not the unbelieving Jews—where the rightful heirs of God's promises. In fact, unbelieving Israelites, born merely of the flesh, were in reality like Ishmael. And just as in Abraham's day Ishmael persecuted Isaac, so in Paul's day, natural, unbelieving Israel was persecuting the true sons of Abraham. Nevertheless, regardless of their fleshly descent, the unbelieving Jew would never inherit the promised Messianic Kingdom.

In spite of what some contend, God does not have two different groups of "elect" people or Saints in the earth: the physical nation of Israel and the Church of Jesus Christ. Some erroneously insist that the true Israel of God and the Church of Jesus Christ are totally separate and distinct entities. According to them, the Church has no legitimate claim to the promises of the Old Testament. The promises God made to Abraham and David rightly belong to natural Israel and can only be lawfully fulfilled to the flesh descendants of Abraham in a future, restored, earthly, Jewish Davidic kingdom.

But the Apostle Paul demanded God only has one body in the earth, the body of Christ, the body of his messianic purpose! He declared the revelation of the mystery of Christ and His Kingdom:

> "So then you are *no longer strangers and aliens*, but you are *fellow citizens with the saints*, and are of God's household..." (Ephesians 2:19-22)

The Gentile believers at Ephesus were no longer strangers and aliens! Instead they had become fellow citizens with the Jewish Saints, of the Kingdom of Heaven. They were fellow members of God's household, the New Israel.

Some have mistakenly taught God revealed to Paul the mystery of the Church. They erroneously insist the Church is an anomaly—an unforeseen and unpredicted parenthesis in God's plan. They demand the Church has no part in the covenants of promise or the Messianic Kingdom. According to them, after the Jews supposedly rejected the Messianic Kingdom which Jesus offered at the time of His triumphal entry into Jerusalem, the Kingdom was postponed until the Second Coming. At Christ's second advent the Messianic Kingdom will again be offered to the Jews. According to this doctrine, following His cross and resurrection, the Lord began to gather a mystical body of believers who will make up the body of Christ—the Church. Once the last person who has been ordained to constitute this invisible body has been added, Jesus will come and secretly rapture or remove the Church out of the world. At this time, God's prophetic time-clock will once again begin ticking. His prophetic program for natural Israel will resume with the appearance of the Anti-Christ and the great tribulation. In the middle of a seven-year tribulation, Jesus will come back to earth and restore the physical kingdom of David and rule Israel and the nations from an earthly throne in Jerusalem for 1000 years, thus fulfilling the promises made to Israel.

The Apostle Paul completely disagrees:

"And by referring to this, when you read you can understand *my insight into the mystery of Christ*, which in other generations was not made known to the sons of men, as *it has now been revealed to His holy apostles and prophets in the Spirit*; to be specific, that *the Gentiles are fellow heirs and fellow members of the body*, and *fellow partakers of the promise in Christ Jesus through the gospel*..." (Ephesians 3:4-6)

Paul's revelation was not that the Church is a mystery. Instead, the mystery revealed to him was that the believing Gentiles are fellow citizens with the believing Jews of the Messianic Kingdom! They are fellow members of the one Messianic body, and fellow heirs or partakers of the Messianic promises in Christ Jesus. Everything God promised Abraham and His seed and everything He promised King David belongs to both Jewish and Gentile believers. Gentile believers are joint heirs with Jewish believers of everything that belongs to Christ!

This was the mystery revealed to the Apostle, and according to Paul, not only to him but to all the holy Apostles and prophets. God does not have two separate and distinct programs for two separate and distinct people. He has been doing one thing throughout the ages—building a people for the

Kingdom. Now, in His Messianic Kingdom, the Son is making one new holy people out of both Jew and Gentile.

The Apostle Paul was emphatic. The promises of God had already been fulfilled. In his own day, the last days of the age of Moses, the Jewish age, the God of Abraham had at long last brought forth the new creation. Out of two previously divided groups—Jew and Gentile—He had made "one new man." He had reconciled them together unto Himself in Jesus Christ. This New Man made up of believing Jews and Gentiles was the Christ, the promised Seed of Abraham, the Israel of God. This New Israel, the Church of Jesus Christ, would be the ultimate instrument of God's Kingdom purpose during the times of the Gentiles to bring all nations under the discipline of God's anointed King until the whole earth has been filled with God's glory.

Throughout the period from the outpouring of the Holy Spirit on the Day of Pentecost until the fall of Jerusalem in A.D. 70, the Apostles went throughout the Roman world gathering the believing remnant of Israelites and the firstfruits of the believing Gentiles. Together they formed the New Covenant People of God, the New Creation, the Body of the Messiah, the New Israel, the Church of the Lord Jesus Christ. Once the work of gathering the remnant and founding the New Nation was complete, the Jewish age came to an end with the destruction of Jerusalem and its Temple.

The burning of Jerusalem and its Temple by the armies of the Roman General Titus signaled the successful completion of the Jewish Mission. It also marked the official beginning of the times of the Gentiles and the Gentile Mission. Just as the Jewish Mission succeeded, so the Gentile Mission will succeed! The nations shall be discipled. The whole earth will be filled with righteousness, peace and joy. All these things shall be accomplished before Jesus comes back again at the Second Coming!

This is the ultimate purpose of the present reign of God's anointed King. Paul proclaimed:

"Therefore it says, 'When He ascended on high, He led captive a host of captives, and He gave gifts to men.'" Now this expression, '*He ascended,*' what does it mean except that He also had descended into the lower parts of the earth? *He who descended is also He who ascended far above all the heavens, that He might fill all things.*" (Ephesians 4:8-10)

This is the apostolically declared purpose of Christ's present reign at the right hand of God. The Lord ascended into heaven and was enthroned to fill all things. The Apostle makes no mention of the Second Coming in this entire passage. The Lord is not coming back at the Second Coming to fill all things. Instead, the purpose of the present reign of God's Anointed King is to fill the earth with the glory of God. Paul declared this would be accomplished throughout Christ's present administration. He boldly proclaimed the Lord's messianic strategy for accomplishing His Kingdom purpose:

"And He gave some as apostles, and some as prophets, and some as evangelists, and some as pastors and teachers, for the equipping of the saints for the work of service, to the building up of the body of Christ..." (Ephesians 4:11-12)

According to the Apostle, the Lord Jesus had already sent forth His anointed servants to gather together the Saints, and form them into the body of the Messiah. The members of this body would be equipped to do His work on earth. The body of Christ would be the instrument of His Kingdom purpose and would succeed in its mission to disciple the nations. As it matures and grows into the full measure of the stature of Christ, it will fill all things.

In keeping with the ancient prophetic theme, the Apostle Paul demanded that before the Lord Jesus returns at the end of history all Satanic rule will be abolished. All devilish power and authority will be subjugated to Christ and His Church in a practical outworking and demonstration of His righteous government of the nations:

> "...then comes the end [the consummation of Christ's Kingdom], when He delivers up the kingdom to God the Father, *when* He has abolished all rule and all authority and power. *For He must reign until* He has put all His enemies under His feet." (I Corinthians 15:24-25)

Jesus Christ is not waiting until some future day to begin to reign. He is reigning now, and must continue to reign "until He has put all His enemies under His feet." When He has fully succeeded in this purpose, then He will deliver up a perfected Kingdom to His Father.

For Paul and his fellow Apostles, there was no talk of a postponed Kingdom or a partial victory. God's Messiah would succeed in His task! He would fully accomplish the Gentile Mission. The Lord Jesus would build His Church, and through His Church all the nations will be discipled.

The sole enemy remaining to be destroyed when the Lord returns will be death.

> "The last enemy that will be abolished is death."
> (1 Corinthians 15:26)

The final victory, victory over death, will await the Lord's Second Coming and coincide with the resurrection of the body. At this time the final judgment will take place. The Lord Jesus will then hand a perfect Kingdom to His Father. Eternity–the perfect age–will begin!

That day on the Mount of Olives overlooking the city, Jesus carefully outlined for Peter and the others the things which would accompany His judgement of Jerusalem and mark the transition from the age of Moses to the age of the Messiah. These things would not only include a period of upheaval and turmoil throughout the Roman Empire with wars and rumors of war, but the appearance of false Christs and false prophets. There would also be persecutions and distress, causing many to fall away from the faith. The Gospel of the Kingdom would be preached throughout the Roman world as a witness gathering the remnant of Israel and enabling the Gentiles to understand the significance of the Lord's judgement which would come on Jerusalem. Daniel's ancient prophecy concerning the Abomination of Desolation would finally be fulfilled as Roman armies surrounded and laid siege to the city, resulting in great tribulation. The Roman siege would end with the destruction of the city.

To insure the disciples would not misunderstand, Jesus declared to them:

> "Truly I say to you, this generation will not pass away
> until all these things take place." (Matthew 24:34)

Jesus was adamant! He left no room for discussion or debate. These extremely important eschatological events would all be fulfilled in the disciples' generation, in their lifetime. They would signify the end of the Old Covenant age and the dawning of the new. According to the Lord, all these things would take place before Peter's generation had passed away.

It all happened just as Jesus promised. All these eschatological events had been fulfilled by A.D. 70. They are not ahead of the Church, as some believe, restricting our progress and keeping us from fulfilling our mission. Instead, they are behind the Church. They are a significant part of our history.

There is nothing yet to be fulfilled, prophetically or eschatologically, in the Olivet Discourse or the rest of the New Testament, before the Church can succeed in its mission. As we stand on the threshold of the twenty-first century, there is nothing to keep the Church from successfully discipling the nations and filling the earth with the glory of God. Jesus is King. His Messianic Kingdom has not been postponed. He is forgiving sin and pouring out the Holy Spirit. He is working with His Church, casting down thrones and raising up thrones.

Charles Spurgeon, speaking of the Holy Spirit's work in relation to Messiah's Kingdom and the discipling of the nations proclaims:

> "I myself believe that King Jesus will reign, and the idols be utterly abolished; but I expect the same power which turned the world upside down once will still continue to do it. The Holy Ghost would never suffer the imputation to rest upon His holy name that He was not able to convert the world."[1]

As Jesus stood that evening before His disciples on the Mount of Olives, He knew who He was. He knew His inheritance. He would not only be the Savior of Israel, but of the world. He would not only be ruler of Israel, but of all the nations of the earth.

He had clearly unveiled His Messianic strategy to His disciples. He had come first for the lost sheep of the house of Israel to redeem them from their sins and fulfill the covenants of promise made to their fathers. After His death and resurrection He would send forth these Apostles throughout the Roman Empire to preach the Gospel of the Kingdom and

---

[1] David Chilton, Paradise Restored: A Biblical Theology of Dominion, (Tyler, TX: Reconstruction, 1985), pp. 129-130.

gather the remnant and the firstfruits of the nations and form them into the New Nation, the Israel of God. But, He had also come as the Lamb of God to take away the sins of the world, establish peace between God and the entire race of Adam, reconcile the whole world to His Father, and pour out the Holy Spirit upon all nations. After the judgment of God upon Jerusalem, He would send forth His apostolic messengers to gather his elect from throughout the four corners of the earth, bring His righteous judgments into the world and fill the earth with the glory of God.

It was a strategy which would consume the disciples. They departed the Mount of Olives that stormy night not knowing all they were about to experience, but staggered by the revelation they received. Their generation would experience the greatest transition in the history of God's creation. Moses was ending and the promised Kingdom of the Son of God was about to be inaugurated during their lifetime. The destruction of Jerusalem and its Temple would be the sign of the Kingdom; the sign on the earth that the Lord Jesus was in heaven reigning as King of Kings and Lord of Lords!

The End!

BIBLIOGRAPHY

Alford, Henry. <u>The New Testament for English Readers</u>. 2 vols. London: Deighton, Bell and Company. 1868.

Barnes, Albert. <u>Notes, Explanatory and Practical, on the New Testament</u>. eds. Ingram Cobbin and E. Henderson. London: James S. Virtue. n.d.

Broadus, John A. <u>Commentary on the Gospel of Matthew.</u> ed. Alvah Hovey. Philadelphia: American Baptist Publication Society, 1886

Carrington, Phillip. <u>The Meaning of Revelation</u>. London: SPCK. 1931.

Chilton, David. <u>Days of Vengeance</u>. Tyler, TX: Dominion, 1987.
<u>Paradise Restored: A Biblical Theology of Dominion.</u> Tyler: TX: Reconstruction, 1985.

DeMar, Gary. <u>Last Days Madness: The Folly of Trying to Predict When Christ Will Return</u>. Brentwood, TN: Wolgemuth and Hyatt. 1991.
<u>Last Days Madness: Obsession of the Modern Church</u>. Georgia: American Vision, 1994.

Edersheim, Alfred. <u>The Life and Times of Jesus the Messiah</u>. 1994; 2nd. reprint ed. Peabody, MA: Hendrickson. 1993

Gibbon, Edward. <u>The Decline and Fall of Rome</u>. Abridgement by D. M. Low. New York: Harcourt, Brace and Company. 1960.

Hobbs, Herschel H. <u>An Exposition of the Four Gospels: Volume 1 The Gospel of Matthew</u>. Four volumes. Nashville: Broadman. 1965.

Josephus. "Antiquities of the Jews". In <u>The Complete Works of Josephus</u>. tr. William Whiston. Grand Rapids: Kregel. 1981. pp. 22-429.

"Wars of the Jews." In The Complete Works of Josephus. tr. William Whiston. Grand Rapids: Kregel. 1981. pp. 429-605.

Keith, Alexander. The Evidence of the Truth of the Christian Religion Derived from the Literal Fulfillment of Prophecy; Particularly as Illustrated by the History of the Jews, And by the Discoveries of Recent Travelers. Philadelphia: Presbyterian Board of Publication. n.d.

Kik, J. Marcellus. An Eschatology of Victory. Phillipsburg, NJ: Presbyterian and Reformed. 1971.

Morgan, G. Campell. Studies in the Four Gospels. Old Tappan, N.J.: Flemming H. Revell. 1931.

Newton, Thomas. Dissertations on the Prophecies, Which Have Remarkably Been Fulfilled at this Time and are Being Fulfilled in the World. 3 vols. 5th ed. London: The Bible and Crown in St. Paul's Church-Yard. 1777.

Pentecost, J. Dwight. Things to Come: A Study in Biblical Eschatology. Grand Rapids: Zondervan, 1958. Words and Works of Jesus the Messiah: A Study of the Life of Christ. Grand Rapids: Academie. 1981

Plumptre, Edward Hayes. "The Gospel According to St. Matthew." In Ellicott's Commentary on the Whole Bible. ed. Charles John Ellicott. 8 vols. Grand Rapids: Zondervan. 1959.

Spence, H. D. M. and Joseph F. Exell, eds. "Matthew." The Pulpit Commentary vol. 15. Grand Rapids: Wm. B. Eerdmans. n.d.

Stagg, Frank. New Testament Theology. Nashville: Broadman. 1962.

Walker, Williston. A History of the Christian Church. New York: Charles Scribner's Sons. 1945

Due